D0441561

Here's to Great Dogs Everywhere.

Many of us would like to believe there's a special place in doggie heaven for the really great ones. I know I want to. No question they've earned it, deserve it, and it seems only fair.

I know there are a great many great dogs out there, working their magic, living their lives with their families and saying it all without ever saying a word. For dog lovers, our precious memories of those "non-conversations" with dearly-departed four-legged friends lend silence a deafening quality.

I explained to a friend that *Paw Prints* is a book about great dogs, not just my dog, although Mac was truly some great dog. And as I've said many times, he was certainly the dog of my life, and his friendship enriched and changed not just my life, but the lives of everyone in our family. While the book is my attempt to capture Mac's remarkably and improbably wonderful story before it fades to past, it's also in many ways my story, too.

Because Mackie and I were happily and deliriously, joined-at-the-paw.

Amazing, I think, that I could learn so much from a guy that never said a word.

Also by Andrew Hessel

Rush to Dawn
The Old Dog's New Trick
Imperfect Resolution
The Do-Over

PAW PRINTS IN MY HEART

Life lessons learned from the dog of my life

ANDREW HESSEL

Copyright 2014

PAW PRINTS IN MY HEART
Life lessons learned from the dog of my life
ISBN: 978-1497595491

Old Dog Publishing
Andrew Hessel
Portland, Oregon
USA

For my wonderful family and dog lovers everywhere.

We're so lucky.

"To err is human,
to forgive canine."

— Anonymous

Contents

Foreword

Paw Prints in My Heart is Mac's story.

I think of it as my gift to our family and all of his friends, two and four-legged, that had the pleasure and the privilege of knowing and being loved by this magnificent old Labrador retriever. It's my best attempt to capture and chronicle a remarkable life, the pain and sadness of his passing, but most of all, his joyful impact upon us over what truly was a most improbable life of fourteen years and a day. A reverent and grateful tribute to a gentle and pure spirit that for me will always be a living reminder of a loving friend in the very truest sense.

In every way, this book was a labor of love and joy to write. Parts will make you laugh, and others may bring you to tears, so a tissue at times may be advised. But I have the highest hopes that you'll read it, enjoy it, and connect in ways that only you can understand. Maybe even share it with friends that might understand and pass it along, as a comfort for a true friend they've lost, and for what they've experienced, and a way for them to remember the laughter and happy times through their tears.

I hope that dog lovers everywhere read this book and see a bit of their dog in Mac.

I hope that the non-dog lovers amongst us read this book and reconsider.

I hope that everyone has at least one dog of their life in their life.

My first novel *Rush to Dawn*, was, in many ways a love letter to my wife, Lynne.

This book, I'd like to believe, is a love letter from Mac to all of us.

The Before and After

I began writing to tell Mac's story, and confess to wondering at times early on why it was so important for me. After all, aren't I just another pledge in the fraternity of grieving pet owners, and Mac, merely another departed furry four-legged friend? And however wonderful he may have been, he was just a dog, right?

On one level, there are the obvious answers to those questions; the common sense truth that for many makes those questions almost rhetorical. But having said that, the truth is I never believed it. Not only was Mac not just another dog, he was, as it turned out, wondrously different and nothing like my three dogs that preceded him; all dogs that I had dearly loved and cried over. But for all that, part of what propelled me forward was to understand the why and what that made him different.

Reason enough to capture his story before time dimmed the memory of it? Maybe. Inevitably, Mac would succumb to the fate of even our most preciously prized memories. What we can count on is time healing but it also steals our memories. I know that's just life, and how it goes. I do get that, and accept it to a point, but something inside wouldn't allow me to just let it happen.

I had to write *Paw Prints in My Heart* and so I have.

But as I began working another question dogged me—forgive the pun but it was like that. Now I was asking myself, okay, he was different, but what was the difference?

The answer would explain two things.

Why I was so driven to tell his story.

And why it's been so profoundly hard getting over losing him.

More than a dog, he was a rare and special friend.

And after all was said and done he gave us wondrous gifts.

But most incredible, life lessons I never could have imagined.

I never thought that much about it at the time, but there was an equality that existed between us, transcending the obvious differences between two-legged and four-legged species. Differences breached by love and camaraderie that was genuine and pure. We delighted in each other's company and never tired of it. In his mind I could do no wrong. I felt exactly the same way about him. He was patient and accepting, trusting and loyal, delighting in nothing more than my company. The truth is I never thought of myself as his owner, and there was nothing conscious about that choice. I suppose it was the natural consequence of being friends and my thinking about that friendship, among other things, in ways I never had before, perhaps trying to understand it better. This business of life; the journey from the beginning to the end.

Friendship follows its own laws and timelines, governed only by the parties constituting it, and known only to them.

Paw Prints In My Heart

I've come to believe every friendship is as unique as a snowflake. The healing and recovery time following the loss of a true friend has no conveniently calculable half-life. Silly as it sounds, to this day Lynne and I still get teary when we talk about Mac. What's changed for me, is that now I'm glad for it.

Mac's improbable life, and perhaps more the improbable relationship we had, has left his paw prints indelibly real and deep in my heart. This book began when I was but a few chapters into my next crime thriller, scratching the surface of a story yet to reveal itself. Mac, my wonder lab, true friend and writing partner, was well into his *Sunset Years*, and I, his vigilant, 24/7/365 nothing-is-too-much-and-mostly-uncomplaining caregiver. When he passed away late in the afternoon on June 14th of 2013, it wasn't before first leaving us his extraordinary Final Gifts. A last reminder of how he'd impacted our lives in ways both expected and unexpected.

Pun intended: Turning the page this time wouldn't be simple or straightforward.

His loss hurt, a lot, more than we imagined in our worst fears. And while it still does, the magic of the old dog's life transcends it. Capturing that magic became a personal imperative.

With dogs we see the pain coming long in advance. Try as we may to steel our hearts for that day, we can't prepare for it. Having always had a dog, I'd been through the loss of them many times before. I loved them all; grieving and crying over each of them. But this time it was so very different and confirmed the truth that I see, now, as a more than fair bargain, albeit a very bittersweet one. A bargain I had no idea I'd made but would make again in a heartbeat.

The greater the gift the steeper the price paid for it, so do be careful what you ask for.

Mac was the finest dog I'll ever know and unquestionably the dog of *my* life. Before him I would have scoffed at the idea that a dog combining Lassie's heart and Old Yeller's steadfast devotion was anything but warm and fuzzy fiction. That he was real and that he was mine is what made saying goodbye so brutally painful and has left a void in our lives I doubt we'll ever fill.

He had a complex relationship with everyone that mattered to him – anyone he met.

While we're over it, in some ways I know we'll never fully get over saying goodbye.

After all this time, I still look for him, and am regularly shocked he's not around.

Not a day goes by that I don't think of Mac and feel thankful for having had him.

Although his final weeks were both ominously sad and inordinately difficult, I'd carried on knowing that I was the luckiest, wealthiest dog lover on Earth. Only when he was gone did I fully understand the flip side of such extraordinary canine fortune. Just like that, I'd become the poorest dog lover on the planet. Such abrupt finality has a stark edge; raw and reeking of sadness and permanence and loss. What I never expected was how fundamentally changed I was by it.

After all, he was just a dog, wasn't he?

We never thought of him that way.

He was Mac. Our friend.

I'd always said I couldn't imagine a house without a dog and meant it. It was true, then.

Now I can't imagine bringing another dog into our family. It shocks me to say it, despite missing having a dog around in all the worst ways and reduced to accosting strangers on the street and politely asking if I could visit their dog on the leash for a little while. I cherish those moments before ultimately backing away. Reminded, yet again, that I'm not ready to take that next doggie plunge.

And as time passes I wonder, more and more, if I ever will be.

About a week after Mac died I published his Tribute Post on my blog. I've included it along with earlier 'Birthday Posts' at the back of the book. It was the writing of that farewell that led to the telling of his story. Writing and sorting through pictures when the wound was freshest, the pain sharpest,

MY COOKIES ARE ON TOP OF THE FRIDGE.

and tears were uncontrollably flowing, began working their therapeutic magic for me. Incredibly, it helped me to get through the worst of it, and although it makes no sense at all, it brought him closer. And knowing that countless dog lovers will understand this all too well spurred me on to finish.

The unexpected story of his tragically-unlucky-but-oh-so-lucky-life should be told.

I'm convinced such a great guy, and such a pure spirit, deserves his own book.

And I write it because for me it's that unfinished business I had to complete.

I mentioned that Mac was my writing partner, but he was also the better half of Old Dog Publishing. He inspired the title and a major character, 'Weller', of *The Old Dog's New Trick*, the second 'Cups Drayton' crime thriller. Weller returned in *Imperfect Resolution*, and as I began writing the next 'Cups' novel, I was bringing him back yet again. It was only after Mac died that I realized before I could write it there was other work to do first.

Mac's story.

Entering our family room an 8 x 10 portrait of Mac in his prime sits in a wooden frame on a small table. With apologies to my three handsome sons, Mac always was the best looking male in our family and had the most magnificent Lab face I've ever seen. To this day my wife, Lynne, can barely look at his picture without crying. I ask her forgiveness and can't thank her enough for allowing it to reside there nonetheless.

Paw Prints In My Heart

She knows I need it there, because for me it's a great comfort.

I pass it countless times each day, often slowing to pat the top of the frame, my hand resting briefly just over his head when I do, murmuring "Mackie ... my baby boy." I grant you it may sound goofy, but somehow, he seems nearer for that, too, and not quite as totally forever gone.

I may never get another dog and I'm prepared should it come to that.

Or, I may wake up one morning burning to begin the hunt.

However it goes, I had to write Mac's story now.

It's my way of saying, "Thanks, Pal."

For leaving your paw prints in my heart.

And much more than that.

CHAPTER ONE
Next Dog Negotiations

This chubby, black block-headed, cute as could be Lab pup would be my fourth dog and I was more than a little excited at the prospect. A furry high-energy bundle of love was a lot to be excited about. I'd soon remember what dog lovers conveniently forget.

It's what our selective memories so considerately hide away. And in doing so removing any reason to delay, spitting in the wind and prompting us to forge ahead and get that next dog. What is it we've all forgotten?

Puppyhood.

As a boy my first dog was a beautiful black and white Springer Spaniel named Bonnie. She was a sweet girl, and a wonderful dog to grow up with. During college my ex-wife and I adopted a magnificent Labrador-Miniature Collie mix I named Dapper that formally introduced me to the wonders of the breed. The marriage didn't make it, but Dapper, my daughter and I became a happy family of three and never looked back.

Dapper had moved west with me, and I took his passing

so hard that I couldn't get a Lab next. I'd remarried and our next dog would join a house full of young children; a liver and white Springer. Ozzie, named after the great Cardinal shortstop Ozzie Smith. I loved him, but he was an oaf without a conscience, putting real pressure on making a better decision with the next dog.

My wife, Lynne, put it bluntly: "I'll divorce you if the next dog is an Ozzie déjà vu."

Don't think she totally meant it, but she had a point and I heard it loud and clear.

"I know you can't live without a dog, I get that," Lynne, said. She measured her words carefully. Since Dapper had died at 14 and a half, I'd only been able hold out about a year before waking up one day and knowing I could wait no longer. I was ready – more than ready – for my next dog. I needed a dog, so I was in the market, knowing that Lynne would be assisting in the process. We'd be taking no chances: doing all we could to beat the odds this time.

"We both know we can't live with another, Ozzie," she continued. "You loved him, and I did, too. He was sweet, but dumb, and impossible so much of the time. Even in his old age he was completely untrustworthy, and that made him hard to live with. You know that, so, *if* we're going to do this, and bring a new puppy into the family," my wife repeated, now very matter-of fact, almost businesslike, "we have to a more educated decision this time."

She had a point, too. Ozzie had … tested us and I can't really say we passed.

Lynne continued. "If you can't live without a dog and have to have one, we'll find a breeder we trust that can help us choose a puppy that can be trained and behave and be a good family dog. He'll be *your* dog, but you know I'll do my part."

"Next Dog Negotiations" were underway.

One of those classic moments of lifestyle bargaining that's a big part of marriage and family life: Terms reached in good faith, but all too often doomed to fail however well intended. In that regard, a new puppy has much in common with a new baby. When a new baby arrives in a household, whoever wears the pants in the family is irrelevant because whoever wears the diapers is the one calling the shots.

Every parent knows that's how it works.

Four-legged new additions wield similar lifestyle-defining powers. Whoever theoretically signed on to be responsible for the new puppy, and of free will agreed to take on the lion's share of the heavy lifting, is replaced by whoever is available to do what has to be done whenever that is and whatever it may be. And depending on the dog, that can be a helluva lot.

In the scheme of things, it's a mad rush from puppyhood to adult doghood, less than a couple of years, and along the way they're impossibly cute wild animals that love us to death while in the early going battling us half to death. They playfully and lovingly wage puppy warfare until they're trained and are abiding by the house rules ... at least when someone's watching.

Many of the rules they help us establish by necessity. Some dogs figure it out and get the rules pretty quickly, while others take longer, and a few just never quite ever get it. Ozzie, our Springer, was one of the latter. Lynne speculated that he was a *mentally defective hedonist* and I could never dismiss that as a real possibility.

Paw Prints In My Heart

The fact is, as a pup he was nuts, and mostly unreachable.
The cute, if over-sized liver and white Springer that had chosen
me at the breeder's, immediately thrust us into survival mode.
Fighting for our lives and in self-defense, his living space
became the laundry room off the attached garage between
the house and the basement level. Not abandoned, not at all,
but banished there until the day, a day we hoped would arrive
sooner rather than later, that he was socialized enough to
actually *live with us*. We really had little choice. With toddlers
in residence in a house with stairs, an out of control puppy
begged disaster.

And Ozzie was out of control.

I decided to give Obedience Training a try, and we went
to classes together. It was no surprise that Ozzie proved to be
not much of student, and after the sixth of eight weekly classes,
despite our earnest practice between them, the instructor kept
us after class and visited with us. She expertly took Ozzie's
lead, and I watched as she worked him herself, and after about
fifteen minutes walked back over and handed his lead back.

"Good luck," she said, failing to hide her doubts from her
eyes.

That night, Ozzie and I became Obedience School Drop-
Outs.

We were waging Puppy Warfare at home and I was on my
own.

Waged on family battlefields, Puppy Warfare typically falls
into three categories.

The Chewing Theater is everywhere and anywhere. The
most common casualties are shoes, usually a pair with a
toe partially eaten from just one of them, and assorted toys,

clothing, personal items, furniture, and, of course, anything even remotely resembling food; all shredded and chewed. To a puppy, all are perceived as fair game because they're there, on their low to the ground radar, and teething puppies chew, some breeds more than others. Ozzie was a helluva chewer. In fact, he once ate almost an entire resin end table before I'd discovered he secreted it behind our shed in the back yard.

The Food Theater is anywhere food of any kind is eaten, prepared or stored. In our case, the Food Theater for Ozzie transitioned as an adult dog to the Begging Theater. Lack of training complemented by my own bad decisions – unwisely slipping him treats during meals early on, doomed us and sealed our fate. While eating something on the couch watching television, I was forced to hold him off with a stiff leg planted firmly against his chest as he strained, whimpered, moaned and groaned disgracefully, single-mindedly focused, eye on the prize.

The Pee, Poop and Puke Theater is the final battlefield, and encompasses the many 'surprises' that appear, usually at the worst possible moment and in the least desirable spots, until a dog is house broken. The unknowns are how long until they get it, how many accidents until they get it, and how permanent and damaging those accidents may be until they get it. In Ozzie's case he was a nominally quicker study than I'd feared given his lack of brain power, although we paid dearly in other ways. I still remember how he baptized new family room carpet when he came home from a kennel with Giardia and left his mark(s) everywhere.

And, because he'd eat anything – indoors and outdoors – he was a big vomit guy, too.

In almost every way, Ozzie really was tough to love.

But love him I did, in spite of himself. He was, after all, my dog.

Unlike his namesake, the classy and slick-fielding shortstop, Ozzie Smith, he was every bit the oaf I jokingly called him. While we laughed about that, the truth is it was well deserved and not all that funny. His greatest life achievement came in elevating begging to an art form and in this endeavor he was as reprehensible as he was determined.

Lynne and I differed in our outrage over his thievery. That he'd steal anything within reach, with no sense of right or wrong. I wasn't at all shocked by this, always considering 'Get Food' as a dog's primary job description. All food is in play and Ozzie played hard and played to win. On the counter, on the table; hell, on your plate, food or anything resembling it, was at risk and he a lawless marauder in pursuit of the spoils of war. The way I saw it, as Lynne never did, Ozzie was dog, an eating machine on a mission, and had a clear edge because he was playing for keeps and couldn't have been more single-mindedly focused.

My previous dogs had been far better behaved and had admirable characters.

My youthful memories of Bonnie were tempered by time. I was sixteen when she'd died at ten, her never quite recovering from what we suspected was poisoning by a neighbor who couldn't abide her occasional escapes from our yard. That was hard to accept.

By the end of my freshman year in college, I simply couldn't live without a dog any longer and found Dapper. Dapper was simply a great dog, truly a wonderful friend and faithful companion who had been nothing short of noble in his senior years. Lynne met him at his most noble and knowing time of life. Ozzie never experienced a noble or knowing time of life.

Right or wrong, my inclination to give my dog slack for bad behavior, and willingly modify my lifestyle to suit any and all requirements that came with ownership, was forged early on. Like an idiot I got a dog in college giving little thought to the consequences and trade-offs to say nothing of the responsibility of owning Dapper.

All I could do was adjust to make it work and accept that, as a college student, having a dog came at great personal cost. I sacrificed much of my freedom and assumed lots of expense, but never once regretted the decision. I was, am and always will be a dog lover. Good thing, too. Housebreaking required me to walk him regularly during frigid Chicago winters from a third-floor walk-up apartment. I'd never recommend it or want to repeat it, but Dapper was more than worth it. And hey, I was young and foolish anyway.

Lynne met Dapper a year before we got married when he was ten years-old. He'd spoiled her and sealed Ozzie's fate. It's fair to say that Dapper was everything that Ozzie wasn't.

Let me tell you that at ten years old Dapper was a smart, savvy, shrewd elder-statesman of a dog, a Yoda-type young dogs came to visit and hang-out with. I swear it's true, he was very cool. Don't let anyone tell you dogs don't know cool. They do, and Dapper was that. Looking back, Dapper must have received a double-dose of the doggie cool gene while Ozzie was hunting for something to eat when they handed them out.

Dapper was the best car dog I've ever known, too. He'd

journeyed out to Oregon with me from Illinois after college, a wonderful road warrior dog on our long cross country road trip together. Perched atop a space I'd carved out for him in the midst of everything I owned stuffed into my dad's old Ford station wagon, he lay in a prone position right behind me and just off of my right shoulder. He loved the car and happily watched the road ahead, giving me an occasional lick on my ear to remind me of his pleasure in the task and his solidarity in the travels west.

A few years later, after settling in Oregon and starting a business with locations in three neighboring cities that required lengthy, daily commutes, our freeway kinship was rekindled. There were a couple of years when we did 50,000 miles a year together. He sat in the backseat on the passenger side, accompanying me day after day, waiting patiently if I was visiting clients, all without a complaint. Nothing made Dapper happier than *getting to go* and he was always ready. When the day came and we put him down at fourteen and a half, I knew that for me getting into the car would never be the same.

Dapper's passing left a huge hole in my heart.

And Ozzie, for all his faults, took a lot of time to get over, too.

Investments of the heart are fairly that way, and I was game for more.

Once I was ready, excitement of a new puppy was shared by our entire family.

We found our breeder, Karen, by chance at one of our oldest son's baseball games in the summer of 1999. She was the mother of a teammate and had bred her two Labs: Abbey, a short, blocky black female and a massive yet rangy yellow male named Oliver, a North American show champion, even. A litter of nine pups – all of them black – arrived on June 13th. Puppies would be available in mid to late August. Good to her word, Lynne wasted no time huddling with Karen and relating our saga with Ozzie. Making it clear what we wanted, and didn't want, in our next dog. Karen promised to study the pups and choose one or two that would fit our family. This was our fighting chance.

In early August we went to see the puppies when they were seven weeks old and they were amazingly cute. She had a cleverly constructed pen under a high deck and mom and her nine offspring were there. The pups exploded out to see us when we showed up and for all their energy and excitement soon lost interest and eight seemed to take off in nine directions. Except for one: a particularly stout little guy that stayed with us, fascinated with us, I think now choosing us. Each puppy had a different colored ribbon around its neck, this one Karen called 'Yellow Boy'.

"He's the one," I told Karen confidently. "He's Mac, and I think he's chosen *us*."

"Funny," Karen replied, "he's built like a Mack truck, a perfect name."

"Yeah," I agreed, "but we aren't naming him after the truck. He's named after Big Mac, Mark McGwire; the Cardinal first baseman. Naming my dog after legendary Cardinals seems to have become a family tradition. If another dog ever comes along, I'll call him 'Yadi' for Yadier Molina, the catcher."

"He was my son's choice for you," Karen said with a knowing smile. "I know you'll all be happy. I brought in the experts to test all of the puppies. They're serious about it, too.

MAC WAS AN ADORABLE PUP.

They've all been checked-out and certified. Mac was quite the hit; they loved his personality and agreed with me that he's something special. He's the pick of the litter."

We were leaving for Lake Tahoe in a few days, and arranged to pick Mac up in two weeks after we returned. He'd be nine weeks old then, and more than ready to leave his mother and litter mates. That year our family vacation had an added undercurrent of excitement. We all looked forward to bringing our new puppy home after ten days in Lake Tahoe.

We prepared, differently than I had with other dogs. Mac would sleep in a kennel, and I kick myself that it took me four dogs to discover the wondrous benefits of crate training. He would be contained at night, in a place of his own where he felt safe and secure, and we could confidently leave him at home unattended without the worry of returning to massive damage. As he grew we went through a few different kennels until we

19

got the XXL.

At nine weeks he was a butterball of Lab pup I could practically hold in my hand. There was no way to know, then, what a specimen he'd become. At his peak, he'd reach almost 120 pounds, the densest hunk 'o dog I ever saw. Like I said before, Mac had an incredibly handsome face, the best Lab face I've yet seen and the best looking male in the family.

Rich, warm brown eyes that suggested intelligence, and he was smart; quickly picking up on the nuances of housebreaking, only needing a couple of guided tours before taking his business to bark-mulched beds along the fence rather than dropping deposits in the grass in the middle of the yard. In the years ahead we would often be amazed at what he seemed to understand, and while that was great, the best part was it never came at the expense of being all dog; a dopey, lovable, gullible dog in all the ways that dogs should be and he warmed our hearts because of it.

All his life people commented on his huge blockhead. As an adult it was bigger than his entire body when we'd first met. He had a prototype English Labrador head accompanied by a deep and broad barrel chest, and an extraordinary tongue with which he used to tender delirious, frenetic doggie kisses. He never shied from showering whoever was available – or within reach with them. And finally, a tail that could do serious damage if it caught you unawares, inches wide at its base and always wagging. I used to call it his 'dinosaur tail'.

He settled in happily, and while he was good from the beginning he only got better. This was a puppy with the optimal puppy's attitude: Happy was his natural state, and he was thrilled to see you and be with you. So often I've joked that while Mac liked other dogs, he loved people. All people; harboring no ill will towards the non-dog lovers among us, confident he'd win them over and he usually did. The truth is he liked everyone and everyone liked him.

Lab puppies aren't passive, energy is never in short supply and they are world class chewers. Mouths are full of razor-sharp teeth and I mean that literally. Chews and bones were Mac's first and favorite pastime, reflecting a genetically encoded need or drive to chew – and as a puppy, to bite. For months my hands and arms were covered with scores of small but not insignificant scabs. Despite loving me immediately and unconditionally, the biting was an inescapable part of this puppy, which I accepted as perfectly reasonable.

We'd get through it and did. Ouch.

Mac displayed a sly side to his personality and a mischievous craftiness once he was old enough to learn chewing had consequences and serious ones, too. Chewing casualties included more than a few personal items, small things such as clothing and books, to much larger – and more costly items – damaged or destroyed after feasting, including pieces of furniture and even a section of the siding on an outside wall I'll explain later.

We'd get upset and then instantly forgive him.

I couldn't stay mad at him, whatever he'd done.

Lynne joked, mostly, that I was harder on our boys than on Mac, and that I'd forgive Mac everything, I'll fess up to that. Guilty as charged; it seemed the least I could do.

After all, he loved me unconditionally in spite of myself, and I returned it.

In our family room there was a wooden coffee table with

an open shelf underneath that, until he outgrew the space, became a cozy spot for a nap or to hang out while the family watched TV. The experience first taught us that 'out of sight, out of mind', really was more than just an old saying. It was one of three classic moments of serious chewing damage done right under our noses.

Tempting, and I suppose tantalizing, round wooden caps covered where the coffee table's legs were connected to the table top. I don't recall how long it took us to realize all four had disappeared, happily, if surreptitiously, devoured while we assumed all was quiet and he was simply being *such a good boy*.

Lynne loved to read the paper in the morning on Adirondack chairs on a back patio, as well as at a wooden table on the other patio, and Mac became her devoted companion, hanging out at her feet. A sweet, loving dog, just hanging out with his mom. Happy to be with her, he was quietly taking advantage of a crack at fresh chewing fodder. The chairs and the table legs of outside furniture would be forever adorned with puppy tooth marks. The scars weren't fatal but they were permanent.

The two tables and the Adirondacks weren't total losses. We laughed at ourselves and had to smile at these items being branded with imprints of puppyhood that would endure long after such a fleeting time had passed. What changed everything for us was more serious damage. Our clothes dryer vents through an outside wall near our kitchen door. For Mac, the warm air from it was an inviting spot for a nap, especially on cool, rainy days, and the siding on that wall around the vent apparently was inviting, too. We discovered later he'd done some serious chewing, but never repaired it. Now it brings a smile and we're glad to have left it.

There was, however, some fatal damage, to the sofa and loveseat in the family room.

While we were absorbed in whatever we were watching or doing, we were more than a little distracted, assuming our puppy was growing up and innocently chilling. Later, reality hit hard. We'd been nothing less than lulled into a false sense of well-being. We'd pay for that. Mac had seized the opportunity and quietly gnawed a corner of the bottom of both the sofa and loveseat; a back leg of the loveseat took a shot that killed it.

I'm smiling about it now, but wasn't so much at the time. But I quickly forgave him, because I'd already fallen head over heels in every way for him. Besides, it was only furniture. The loveseat didn't survive and had to be replaced. By then we had learned about Bitter Apple, a miraculous product to combat chewing, and a product everyone should add to the surviving-a-puppy-tool box. Unfortunately, we'd learned about it a bit too late.

CHAPTER TWO
Early Warning Signs

At ten months and with Mac's first birthday in sight, we couldn't have been happier as a family. We'd fallen in love with him and he'd not only fallen in love back but he'd fallen hopelessly, and that made everything all the more fun. Everyone in the family was happy and having an absolute ball with Mac. With this amazing Lab we were now a happy family of seven.

At six months I'd told Lynne, "Mac is the finest dog I'll ever know" and she asked, "How do you know?" "I know," I said, "I just know." And I just did, I knew.

But there was trouble ahead.

Some things just weren't right.

Not that Mac wasn't all dog in all the right ways, he was. He was a cerebral dog, yeah, but a cartoon dog at the same time. Because of it he made me laugh every day, and that was a gift. A gift I swear I would continue to receive until his last days and it means even more to me now that he's gone. But for all the happy stuff, there were mitigating factors. A number of disturbingly uncharacteristic and un-puppy-like aspects to his behavior.

Paw Prints in My Heart

First, Mac was the Labrador retriever that wouldn't retrieve, quickly figuring out that it wasn't in his best interests and wisely passing. This wasn't for our lack of trying. We'd throw a ball and he'd tear after it and bring it back; once. If we repeated the process, he might bring it back a second time. But we soon let go of any dreams of our family in the back yard or on the beach with our All American dog fetching non-stop and never tiring of it. For us, that was simply never meant to be. The norm for Mac became fetching the ball once, and the second time catching up with it safely out of range at the other end of the yard, thinking better of it and laying down.

Clearly, this was not normal, but I rationalized it as just one of those quirky things – no stranger to avoiding the unpleasant when possible or convenient. Telling myself, assuring myself as the rationalization guru I can be at times, yet this time never quite able to sell myself that on any level this was reasonable, that this could be explained. No biggie, I wanted to believe. He's healthy, we thought, and happy, we knew. And, after all, he was the pick of the litter. Putting it to the back of our minds and living with it for the moment so we didn't steal from the moment.

Hey, maybe some retrievers simply don't retrieve. That was possible, wasn't it?

I wanted to believe it was and find a way to explain away our disappointment that the All American staple of a dog fetching a ball or stick – such great fun, great exercise, and part of any healthy Lab's profile – simply wasn't, and wouldn't ever be, part of his. I convinced myself that wasn't implausible.

But other things weren't so easy to rationalize away.

Mac loved walks and we started each day with one after

breakfast. As was so often the case, doing something once set a new precedent and he embraced our early morning walk immediately with unbridled enthusiasm like a sacred time-honored tradition. Any thought I had of lazy mornings and putting the walk off until later simply wasn't tolerated. This was one of the few things he was adamant and insistent about.

On the rare occasions when I tried to deny or postpone the walk, it was instantly made clear he had other ideas and gave me no choice. He'd sit, quietly at first, directly in front of me, eyes glued on me and boring virtual holes in me. Over the years we saw him become less patient in this instance, with a quicker transition to antsy, and flinching with my every movement. Leaving no doubt that it was time, he was more than ready, and totally perplexed that I wasn't. In old age, out of impatience and incredulous at our negligence, he'd leapfrog past the preliminaries, stand and bark at me. And he had a booming bark that was sure to catch your attention.

I often wondered if it woke the neighbors.

As a puppy, our morning walks had two very distinct halves. As his first birthday neared, he was well on his way to becoming a really big boy, over a hundred pounds, and walking him in those days was no leisurely stroll. Trembling with excitement when he saw me leash in hand, exploding through the open door with astounding energy – on the first part of his walk.

I was charmed by his excitement, and often he'd hurry along taking the lead in his mouth, like he was in charge and walking me, and challenging me with a tug-of-war. I loved his spirit and many times gave in and let him 'walk me' for a while until he lost interest in it. He always did because he had more important things to do; there was everything to sniff-out and territory to mark and claim. I often found myself holding on for dear life with him dragging me down the street. And I'm a big guy, I'll never tip the scales south of two hundred again, and it was a battle: Think walking a fullback.

If this *first* part of our walks was characterized by his boundless energy, enthusiasm and brute strength, the back half of our early morning constitutionals was memorable for the utter lack of all of the above returning home. The back half of our walks was the mirror opposite of the first half. He was in no hurry, slowing way down practically to a crawl. Increasingly, I'd be walking along, lost in my thoughts, only to get rousted from my mental meandering, like a dog walking cartoon character jolted by the sudden and unexpected discovery of pulling on dead weight and ending up flat on his back Looney Tunes-style; a couple of times I nearly did. I'd turn and find him smiling weakly but sitting down behind me, having come to a complete halt, as if saying it was time to stop. This couldn't be the same dog that had bolted out the door dragging me behind, but it was. I was left no choice but to coax him forward and the return home was a perplexing process of stops and starts. Many days he was limping when we finally arrived, and indoors he'd immediately lie down, by all appearances exhausted and spent from the walk.

Lynne suggested that he knew the route we took and might have his own agenda.

"He knows you're heading home and slowing down is his way of extending his walk."

Maybe, but I doubted that. Tempting to consider, though recognizing it as a great rationalization opportunity. But even my rationalization skill didn't allow accepting that explanation for such odd behavior from a puppy.

So I looked for something with more persuasive teeth, and speculated, "Maybe he's growing so fast that he has *growing pains* or gets tired out."

Yeah, right – our puppy was "tired" after a walk.

As soon as the words came out of my mouth I knew how absurd they sounded. I wanted something simple and benign to explain what made no sense at all, and at that point didn't consider that something was seriously, chronically and life-threateningly amiss.

No, this was big time denial. Subconsciously, I may have suspected the truth but I was unwilling to confront the unpleasant reality and chose to invent implausible explanations. In my heart I wanted to believe, but in my head I didn't buy either explanation – Lynne's or my own – and as it turned out for good reason.

Neither was correct.

A major league wake-up call came when Lynne ran into a neighbor on her morning walk and stopped to chat. Her friend remarked that she'd passed Mac and me walking a few mornings and noticed that his right rear leg looked crooked, almost bowed. Blinded by infatuation, I guess I'd missed that, or hadn't ever seen it from far enough behind to notice, or didn't *want* to see it. I remedied that right away with a close look and didn't like what I saw. Sadly, she was right and although I didn't know what it all meant, I knew it wasn't good.

In March, three months before his first birthday, our family was making a Spring Training pilgrimage to Florida to see the Cardinals get ready for the 2000 season and we'd have to board Mac. We learned of a kennel on Sauvie's Island outside of Portland that specialized in Labs and also offered obedience training.

Why lie?

I had zero desire to become a two-time Obedience School Drop-out, so I jumped at the chance for a turn-key-twofer. Mac would be trained while I drank beer, watched baseball and soaked up the sun enjoying Spring Training in Florida. Everyone I knew back home in Oregon was soaking up *liquid sunshine* where the only sign of spring was on the calendar and left you wondering, as we do in so many years, if the rains would ever end.

Bad news was waiting when I picked Mac up.

There had been no Obedience Training. Mac was limping badly and they'd made the right decision to let him rest, without stress, physical or mental. Anticipating learning about what we believed was a bad leg, we'd already scheduled an appointment with our vet. Bad leg, bad hip or whatever the issue turned out to be, we'd deal with it.

I took him in the next morning.

I was with him, of course, as he was examined, and after only a quick look at him walking, he was quickly moved to an examination table – a large one – and that's where things got interesting. My vet used his fingers, probing the leg and hip, feeling presumably for abnormalities. He didn't say much, aside from cryptic grunts and "hmms". When he finished, he brought my dog down to floor, gave him some treats, and I awaited the verdict.

"I'm referring you and Mac to a specialist; they're the best with this kind of thing, orthopedic issues. Here's the name of the surgeon I want you to see. I'm pretty sure the issue is his hip but the diagnosis needs more expertise in this area than I can give you. Let me know how it goes, and good luck," Dr. P said with a tight smile.

I was surprised, but only a little and not rocked by it.

We already knew there was a problem and I'd researched hip dysplasia and suspected that meant surgery, assuming fixing the problem would require going under the doggie knife. So, the salesman in me rationalized the upside as expediting the inevitable process; sooner rather than later seemed better, so let's get to it.

Mac was not quite ten months old at the time.

A couple of days later we saw Dr. H. the vet at the referral clinic.

I'll refer to our wonderfully kind legion of vets by their initials; to protect their privacy.

Dr. H. was a wonderful guy, a little younger than me, so not a kid; but inordinately knowledgeable and consummately experienced. The clinic had a different feel, too. One side was the general clinic, but we were on the referral side. This, I would come to discover, was the *check your wallet side* where the big problems with dogs and cats were addressed with big efforts, the latest medical technology and big bucks.

He watched Mac walk from different angles, and varying distances, and then kneeled down and felt him all over. Mac rewarded him with kisses for the soft words the doctor spoke to him. This was all part of the process that would determine where we'd go from there.

Next came full body x-rays. Dr. H. wanted to see *every* joint.

The pictures would be taken the following morning under general anesthetic.

Apparently there were many needed and some with difficult but essential angles; it was the only way. The plan was nothing to eat or drink after dinner that night. I'd bring him in the following morning and he'd spend the day. When we picked him up late afternoon we'd hear the doctor's findings and recommendations. For one of the few times in all the years to follow, I had a conflict I couldn't resolve. Big corporate honchos were in town and that meant meetings and the mandatory meaningless dinner glad-handing the senior execs.

Lynne would pinch-hit for me and retrieve our retriever that didn't retrieve and now was struggling just to walk. She'd get the news from Dr. H. and fill me in, which I thought would be when I got home. But my phone rang while I was sitting in the bar having drinks before dinner. Answering the call I heard her sobbing.

She was so upset I couldn't understand what she was saying. I got up from my seat at the bar and walked out into the hallway and found a quiet space where I could listen to her without distraction, hoping to calm her down and get the gist. What I learned would change our lives fundamentally for more than the next decade.

Lynne compared what Dr. H. had told her to a bowling ball shot to the gut.

"I broke down hearing it, listening to the long list of

31

problems that went on for what seemed like forever. He just kept going and going and it got worse and worse. Then he spelled out the options: If we do nothing, he'll be crippled, toast, unable to walk in a year or two. So I started to cry and couldn't stop and all they had for me to wipe my eyes was rough paper towels. They helped us into the car and I just sat there. Mac was fine, licking my ear from the back seat, but I was in shock. Total shock and I couldn't move. We just sat in the car."

The bottom line was that Mac didn't have a bad leg.

He had four bad legs.

All his joints were bad. Later Dr. H. would explain it matter-of-factly: "He just wasn't put together right," and I remember thinking so much for the 'certification' our breeder had paid for when Mac and his littermates had been examined by the 'experts'.

"Did he say what he'd do?" I asked Lynne.

"I asked him that," she assured me. "His perspective is very different. Not just that he's a vet and sees this kind of thing every day. Dr. H. told me he grew up on a farm, and when animals weren't right they put them down. Just like that, put him down. But there are surgical options that weren't available for problems like these even a few years ago," she finished, and then fresh sobbing began.

When I calmed her, she asked, "What are we going to do? This is Mac ..."

"I'm calling the clinic right now to make an appointment for tomorrow, whenever they can get me in. You're welcome to come with me, but I'll understand if after today's visit you're so beat up you'd rather take a pass and hear it from me."

"You won't … we can't … "She didn't finish the thought and I got the implied question.

"We aren't there, yet. I don't know enough. I've got questions. Starting with what's possible? What does surgery entail? What does it mean? But the real question is can he have an acceptable quality of life? Without those answers I really don't know enough, other than I feel like crying."

But that wasn't quite true; I knew two things beyond doubt.

The entire family, all of us, had fallen head over heels in love with Mac.

And he returned that love so totally that he was not only the dog of our lives, but I'd also come to believe with all my heart that he was the best dog *I'd* ever know. He was already the *happiest* dog I'd ever known. An ever-present smile, he delighted in *everything* and brightened every day for us. This dog loved life and loved his people. Whatever his pain, and I'd come to understand that it was considerable, and for the resulting limits on running and playing all day as is a puppy's job description, nothing dimmed his happiness with us or ours with him.

The idea of putting him down was unthinkable. What I did, at home and at work, was to solve problems. There was always a way, even with the biggest and most insoluble problems. This one was a big one and certainly didn't have a handy quick fix solution, but how big I didn't yet know. I did know that I was unwilling to give up without exploring every possibility.

The next afternoon I met with Dr. H. and got the answers.

"Hips, knees and a problem with the right rear leg that

might require a stainless steel rod to straighten and stabilize it. It's seriously bowed. But the front legs are even worse; the elbows."

"Can you do these surgeries?" I asked.

"I can do the rear legs, I'm totally confident with hips. There's a surgeon in Eugene, Dr. S. He has pioneered hips, breakthrough techniques and innovations. Amazing stuff that's led to human orthopedic advances; I'm serious when I say that there's no one like him. In recent years he's brought in surgeons like me from across the country and taught us his techniques," he said.

In many respects, this was great news. Five years earlier this wasn't possible.

"What about the front legs?"

"Dr. S. is still refining those procedures, for the elbows, and I'd recommend him for that. When the time comes, we'll contact him and schedule, but for now, if you decide to proceed with this, we start with the hind legs." At that point he rattled off medical terms I can't remember and didn't matter to me, referring to bones and joints and surgical techniques. My eyes rolled as my heart broke.

"What's involved in the surgeries?" I asked, and braced for the answer.

"He's under, obviously, and will spend a day or two here, after each one. He'll be bandaged and have stitches, staples, and the shaved leg and hip will look awful for a while. Medication for pain, antibiotics and keeping him off his leg as much as possible, of course."

"What about activity?" I followed up.

"His activity has to be strictly limited and controlled, no

option with this. In and out on his leash only – to take care of his business – for eight weeks, until Mac is stabilized and healed … It won't be easy," Dr. H. conceded. "he's a high-spirited puppy."

"That's an understatement," I said, "this is a Lab puppy were talking about. Okay, now I have to ask. It's not about money, but how much? What are we talking about?"

"I'll ballpark it at $3000 to $4000 per leg."

I closed my eyes, rubbed my temples, and asked, "If we do it, I know he won't be fixed, he won't be *normal*; but can he live a happy life? Will he be able to get around, go for walks, can he … be a dog? To me, that's it, that's the tipping point."

Dr. H. smiled, a little.

"He'll never pass through Airport Security, become an Olympic athlete or a Show Champion, but he'll have a life. If you're willing to take this on, and make no mistake this is a major commitment, he'll have what Mac really needs … you. One more thing I have to add for what it's worth. I don't say this usually, but what a personality. He's really a great guy."

"I'll look at my schedule and discuss it with Lynne. We'll get back to you in a couple of days to schedule the first surgery."

I stood and slowly walked out of the office.

The next *leg* of the adventure was about to begin.

CHAPTER THREE
If you'd known then, would ya?

Some choice: We could do the unthinkable and put him down, or instead we could do the unthinkable and try to fix him and hope for a happy ending that was in no way a certainty.

The latter meant a couple of years of surgical adventures, intensive recuperation, all coming at a cost that made you question your sanity.

Like we had a choice. Common sense, money, whatever, the fact is that putting Mac down was simply unthinkable and I never once seriously considered it. Mac was family and in less than a year had brightened our days and added to our lives in ways we'd fight to keep.

"What's the plan?" Lynne asked, "Do we have one?"

Both more than reasonable questions, I thought, wishing, and not for the first time, I had more definitive answers.

So without hesitation I answered. "We'll take it a day at time, and one surgery at a time, working through all four legs." I answered, knowing we were both as ready as we could be but also blissfully ignorant and unprepared because there was no

real way to anticipate what the future would actually look like.
We were flying blind.

Fortunately or not, we would find out how things would
be when we got there.

What we could expect was initially some heavy Florence
Nightingale duty, serious meds and then ongoing caregiving.
As dog owners we were fully engaged on a big time level. Far
more than we had bargained or signed on for in every way.
But never was there any doubt of what we would do for this
dog. With an unspoken understanding of what we never
articulated, the fact was that Lynne and I both considered Mac
not just part of the family, but our fifth child.

For the foreseeable future, although he was housebroken
and approaching the end of puppyhood, Mac wouldn't be
the turnkey dog we'd let in and out at will. We'd not only be
engaged big time, but for a long time it was going to be all the
time. And that, as it turned out, was the easy part.

For the next two and half years, our lives would be part of
a canine orthopedic quest.

The single most amazing thing was throughout all of it, it
never changed Mac's spirit.

The second most amazing thing was that I never minded
what I had to do.

I only wanted him to get through it.

What we couldn't know until we were into it was what
getting through it would mean.

I didn't know that over the next thirty months, there
would be not four but five major leg surgeries. During this
time unexpected issues arose and circumstances changed,
some of those things beyond our control. And since the

process wasn't as linear as I'd hoped, at times we had to get creative and improvise. At a critical moment, a key surgeon became unavailable and that completely upended the plan, causing me to scramble and gamble and question my sanity more than once. The impact of it all on our daily lives was considerable. Temporary adjustments became temporarily permanent adjustments. These became the new normal in our lives, tinged by both guarded optimism and fearful pessimism.

There were no guarantees other than time, trouble and lot of dollars.

We could go through it all and it still might not be enough.

After each surgery, recuperation with Mac was limited to going in and out on his leash and only to take care of biz for the first eight weeks. No walks and no play. Multiply this times his five surgeries (the right elbow had to be performed a second time) and that's a total of forty recuperation weeks, nearly a full year. After the first eight weeks, recuperation and stabilization would be ongoing. We had to be cautious and careful, avoiding complacency and risks because this would be a lengthy process working through the joints in all four legs. At the beginning, feeling our way, getting to the other side of our Mac's orthopedic dilemma couldn't have seemed farther away. Like being tossed into the deep end of pool and learning via the sink swim method.

But it was his only chance. And making the most of that chance required doing whatever we do along the way to safeguard his legs until all four were done. Then, hopefully, stabilized, strengthened and recovered to whatever his new physical normal was going to be. I never really thought of it as protecting our investment, but the dollars were big enough to make me chuckle more than once and wonder why I didn't. The focus was on doing all we could to give the dog we loved a chance at a good life and keep him in our lives.

So at not quite a year old, Mac became the puppy that physically couldn't ever be allowed to be a puppy. We had to monitor and be aware of his outside activity, and that became part of everyone's business and was soon woven deeply into our family fabric. To varying degrees, we all become not just dog owning dog lovers, but engaged caregivers.

And I was our leader, taking the medical and nursing point, facing the first surgery.

I felt sad thinking about denying Mac his freedom as part of his lifestyle for the next couple of years, and couldn't help feeling guilty about it as we did, despite knowing we had no choice. I privately worried that it could crush his spirit. Turn him into a sad sack or worse, not to mention that he was now going steady with the vet, and all of that had to take its toll. He'd be cut, poked, stabbed, jabbed, stitched, stapled, sedated and shaved, and getting through one surgery would be met with only the briefest tempered celebration because the next one would be looming ever closer.

I feared that with each operation I'd wonder if this would be the one that would break him, and if the aggregate toll of surgical high jinx would understandably finally be too much, but it never was. Mac would prove to be an amazing patient, indomitably positive and always making the best of it. He seemed to understand, in some way, that this was his chance and he never complained.

He accepted everything good-naturedly, and there was a lot to accept. As a breed Labs are known to be remarkable stoics, and Mac demonstrated that admirably over the years. I'd often marvel that while living in constant pain, he never showed it, never let it diminish his love of life, or change in any way the affection he had for everyone he met every day of his life.

I truly admired that.

"Who would have thought a dog could make me feel ashamed for complaining and moaning and groaning about my aches and pains," I remember telling Lynne once.

"Or that in spite of all his pain and trouble, he makes it a non-issue and can be so utterly happy and trusting of life," she replied.

Less than two weeks after the diagnosis, Mac went under the knife for his right rear leg, and we began the once unimaginable orthopedic journey. In his kennel was fresh bedding and I'd purchased a sling for times he'd need help to get up and down and go in and out. I'd asked Lynne to stock up on cheddar cheese, cream cheese and turkey hot dogs as these would comprise my first attempts at creating crafty pill-bearing vehicles for his meds.

The night before the first surgery and sensing something was up, he cast me a baffled and perplexed look, a theatrical astonished and hurt look that we'd forgotten his dinner. I thought he pulled the abused innocent victim thing off rather well, but he quickly moved on. He was clever, it struck me then, as it would so many times in the years ahead, how easily he could manipulate me, how skillfully he did it, and that I was such a willing dupe. The truth is I liked it and gave into it, willingly. That fact led to a discussion Lynne and I had many times over the ensuing years.

"You get mad at the kids for the most insignificant things – and me, too – but you never, ever, get mad at Mac. Your dog can do no wrong, and sometimes we can do no right," she would say, almost playfully but there was no mistaking or escaping the truth of it. She'd nailed me.

"Yeah, Dad, you like him best and Mac is your *favorite* son," our three boys echoed her sentiments – half-kidding and piling on for the fun of it and because they could.

Ouch. They had a point, but I reminded them that in some ways we all felt that way.

"Well," I said, "I think we all like him best. Let's face it: he's the most agreeable, he never complains, accepts us completely, loves us unconditionally and all he wants is to be with us. You can't deny that's kinda hard to find fault with!"

Bright and early next morning, I took him in to the vet.

As always, Mac was thrilled to see everyone.

The truth is that of the two of us, I was the emotional one; he was fine. I said goodbye, a little tearfully, but he was so excited and happily distracted with new people that all I got was a quick lick as he was led merrily out of sight. Mac acted like he was going off to camp. I was told to call them anytime for updates. He could conceivably go home tomorrow, but depending on how things went might stay over another night, if he needed it, or if we preferred it.

I'd done the math, and had thought a lot about the process that I believed then would be four surgeries and recoveries; the more I thought about it, two, maybe closer to three years seemed right. On the other side he'd be an adult dog, his puppyhood lost. At the same time, he was a dog and knew none of that. We'd find out if even Lab stoicism had its limits.

After the early morning surgery, I was updated mid-afternoon that he'd come through it just fine. The first milestone would come the next morning. When it did, it was the great news I'd hoped for, all things taken into account; he was a little dopey and a whole lotta happy.

Everyone at the clinic loved him; he was charming all the techs and the docs noted his remarkably positive attitude. None of which surprised me. Mac was a people-first dog in every way and being happy with his lot was indeed his way. Besides, all the docs and techs were a new audience for him to charm and he made the most of it. By late afternoon they had made the decision to keep him another night, and I liked the fact that we'd be bringing him home one more day removed from surgery, and a day stronger.

The next morning I picked him up and brought him home along with a big bag of meds: Antibiotics, pain pills, a sedative to keep him quiet if needed and a cleaning solution to use on his stitches and staples along the incision lines.

They'd done the right hip, as well as inserting a stainless steel rod in his leg to straighten it. I got a little teary – which is my way – but he really was quite a sad sight. Not just for sore eyes, he looked like he'd been to war. Still, he was happy and absolutely thrilled to see me, albeit a bit worse for wear, and seriously shaved to the skin on his leg and much of his backside. All in all, pretty ghastly looking with the stitches, staples and the bandages.

The first day of a new daily routine discovered on the fly we'd follow for the next eight weeks and then design the next new routine for the next phase after that. I hoped if we were smart, and careful, we find a way for a *little more* dog stuff, but the emphasis was on a little more. Controlled, strictly limited and we'd be watching over him – until all four legs were done.

What we didn't get throughout it all were any complaints from him.

Mac was a model patient and didn't cry, whimper, moan or groan, agreeably going with the flow we kept trying to find. There was, however, one small area where he resisted and that forced me to get creative.

He wasn't a fan when it came to taking pills, one of the few things he was uncooperative about and battled a little. I wasn't a fan of prying open his jaws and then jamming them down his throat. And for the first few weeks after each surgery there were going to be quite a few pills, so I began the hunt for the optimal 'hiding vehicle'. I started with cheese, cream cheese and peanut butter, but soon discovered they were far too messy as evidenced by our family room carpet. Inventor mode launched me on my way to an accomplishment I'm actually rather proud of; what became known in our family as *peanut butter bready balls*.

I'd had a few failed attempts, despite thinking I had been rather clever with them. With high hopes I experimented briefly with turkey hot dogs. Slipping a pill into a hunk of meat I knew he'd inhale without chewing, hit me as an absolute natural, a no-brainer. After all, when it came to food he was an eating machine. I saw this as my clear window of opportunity. Sensing my imminent success, I confess that I was rather pleased to think I was smart enough to outsmart my dog.

Mac, as it turned out, had other ideas.

Turkey dogs worked once.

The second time I tried it, I found one of those very

expensive antibiotic capsules lying on the carpet, and had to resort to jamming it down his throat. I watched him closely the next time to understand where I'd gone wrong. It was pretty funny, too. Observing Mac delicately, gingerly, eating around the pill, swallowing the hot dog and spitting out the medicine brought a smile but forced me to continue my pursuit of what would work.

Shocked to think that I was giving up on hot dogs, which a day before had seemed so perfect, I was now banking on his *love* of peanut butter, and created what indeed became the perfect pill-bearing vehicle I'd use for the next thirteen years. A small piece of bread with peanut butter and the pill rolled up together – and like magic, gone in an instant. The fact is I realized that he would have done the same and devoured *anything* with peanut butter.

We made it through the first surgery and recovery, all of that during late spring and early summer – and the time of year was a real help because we didn't have to battle the elements and worry about keeping him dry as we would have during the winter. Hoping for similarly favorable weather, I pushed ahead with the surgery on his left rear leg and in late summer he went in.

The constant with Oregon weather is that it's consistently inconsistent. The rainy season might mostly hold off through the initial eight weeks of in-and-out on his lead, or not. I could only hope to get lucky. But even if the weather didn't treat us kindly, we had reason to be more upbeat. We were now post-surgery doggie care veterans.

At least this time we knew what to expect.

"If you'd known what this would be like would we be

doing it?" Lynne asked with a smile.

Don't you love rhetorical questions?

On the plus side, the second surgery was only the hip, a simpler and comparatively straightforward procedure unlike the first surgery that had been complicated with the steel rod. We did it, got through it, and it was about halfway through recuperation that I began looking ahead to formally plan for his front legs.

Unfortunately, Dr. H. couldn't do them, and that was both a disappointment and a concern. I'd developed such great respect for his skill and genuinely liked him as a person and, I thought in an odd way, a co-conspirator on the quest.

He'd grown to genuinely like Mac, too, telling me one day, "You know what I like best about Mac, he's a great guy," repeating what he'd said at our first meeting, "I've poked him pretty seriously and he holds none of it against me."

"He won't," I said, "holding it against you isn't in him. What Mac has is an amazing will to live and a love of life, a trust of life."

I confess that it warmed my heart knowing a vet that sees dogs by the gazillions could see in Mac the remarkable spirit and people-centric personality I did. It was, as well, a kind of confirmation for the lunacy guiding me down this surgical highway without passing judgment of any kind.

Anyway, we'd be hitting the road for the next surgeries, because when it came to doggie elbows, only Dr. S. in Eugene did them. With a referral from Dr. H. I wasted no time and was booking a date for surgery #3, the first elbow, in late April, with an eye on late summer for the second one.

Which wasn't a bad plan, but it never had a chance to work.

Early in the New Year, Dr. S's office called and again I had to get creative.

"Mr. Hessel? I'm calling from Dr. S's office in Eugene."

"Hello," I said with real enthusiasm that would soon be summarily crushed.

"I'm afraid we're going to have to cancel Mac's surgery," the voice began.

This was the last thing I expected, and the truth is I was rocked by it. "Can we reschedule?" I asked.

"Not now, and I'm not sure when that might change," was the reply.

"Wow," was all I could muster, wondering what we'd do.

"Doctor S. isn't well and we're not accepting any appointments at the moment. There's nothing we can do. I'm so sorry for the inconvenience and hope you'll find another surgeon. If things do change, we'll let you know."

I think I said thank you and wished Dr. S. well, but my head was spinning.

Two things were immediately clear.

Reading between the lines, I knew Dr. S. had to be seriously ill. And we were back to square one.

But unlike the hips, this was worse than square one.

No one else did elbows.

Two days later Mac had a check-up and I put the question to Dr. H.

"Dr. S. has cancer," he told me. "I just heard. It's lousy luck. He brought surgeons in from all across the country and taught them his hip techniques. Since then, elbows have been his work in progress, and he was planning to bring us in again to teach us what he's figured out. Now it looks like that isn't going to happen, might not ever happen."

"So what can we do? I'd always assumed that the front legs, his elbows, were even more critical. Without doing them what we've done won't matter, because he'll lose all mobility and the clock is ticking. There must be someone else."

"Maybe there is someone," Dr. H. replied, thoughtfully stroking his graying beard. "But understand this. I'm not exaggerating when I say Dr. S. knows more than any of us – don't discount the risk with anyone else."

"Look," I blurted out, "I don't expect a guarantee, I'll settle for a shot and at this point, I'm willing to gamble and will bear the risk. Any risk as far as that goes, so I'm taking that off the table and off you, okay? We're halfway home and it's more than a little late to stop now, and I won't let it end here. In for a penny, in for thousands of pounds, I guess, and I won't go quietly. Tell me, please, who are you thinking of?"

"Dr. L., he's got a referral clinic in Clackamas. He was part of the group that learned the hip techniques and I know he's done some elbows, and has some ideas of his own. A bit of a drive for you, thirty miles or so. You're good with that?"

"Are you kidding? Eugene was over a hundred miles, so I just saved a lot of time and won't need a hotel."

He nodded in agreement. "If you like, I'll call over there today and give Dr. L. a summary of what we've found and what I've done and tell them to expect to hear from you," he said, his voice trailing off.

"Make the call, and tell them I'd like to get Mac in to see him right away."

When I called they were ready for me, too.

"Dr. L. gave me instructions for you," the assistant told me.

"Wow, that's great," I said, impressed already.

"He wants all of the X-rays Dr. H. took. I'll make the call and arrange it for you."

"No problem, I'm happy to do that," I answered. Hey, given what they'd cost I was thrilled to get double-duty from them. "Is there anything else?"

"Yes. He wants an MRI to see inside the joints. There's a facility we use in our center just across our parking lot. You could have it done and bring it with you for your appointment."

So much for the double-duty I thought.

Doggie MRI's must cost a bundle, but what did that matter? I was doing my best not to keep a running tally in my head, it wasn't about money. Still, the dollars were mind-numbing. The thought occurred to me that each leg cost more than my first car.

So, that day we saw two new vets, at the MRI Clinic and Dr. L's Referral Clinic.

Mac, of course, was in heaven, making new friends and loved everyone at both places.

I kept expecting him to get wary, looking for signs that it changed him. Given what he'd already been through he'd more than earned the right to balk at anything resembling a vet, but he never did. Ever. Not once. And for all the rest of his life he never would, which was a blessing of sorts, because there was so much to come.

Leaving Mac in the car, I walked the x-rays inside and took care of the business.

Dr. L. would look at them while we were at the MRI Clinic that was more than a little high-tech impressive. I was about to find out that the cost of a doggie MRI made the full body x-rays seem a relative bargain. Afterwards, with the MRI on a disk, Mac and I went in to meet Dr. L. Outside he watched Mac walk from different angles and distances. This was followed by a comprehensive examination with him moving Mac's joints, rotating them in different ways and feeling in and around them with his fingers. He didn't say much, although his silence was occasionally punctuated with a crinkled brow and unintelligible mutterings.

"Let's go into my office and look at the MRI. I've had it copied to video tape so we can play it on the VCR and look at it on a bigger screen."

In those days, DVDs were in their infancy and DVRs not yet available, so for the times it was about as high-tech as it got. What I saw reminded me of *Fantastic Voyage*, a bad 70's movie about a doctor in a submarine, micro-sized and injected into a patient's bloodstream battling evil white blood cells that became horrifying adversaries. All I really knew was that I had no idea what I was looking at and Dr. L.'s medical explanation lost me immediately with names of bones, medical conditions and surgical procedures I knew nothing about. My gut told me none of it was good, however. When the tape ended, Dr. L. confirmed that suspicion.

"I'm going to give it to you straight. These are simply the worst elbows I've ever seen from a cartilage standpoint," he said.

"Why is that?" I asked.

"Mac has no cartilage. None; the joints are bone on bone.

The poor guy must be in constant pain, but these Labs never show it. And he's such a big boy; I'm amazed he gets around as well as he does. There is little doubt that without surgery he won't be able to for much longer. I'm sure you know that; that's what brought you're here. And the upside isn't all that good because whatever we do, the cartilage problem can't be corrected. There simply isn't any and that won't change. He'll live with the pain always, whether we improve his mobility or not."

"Look," I interrupted. "I know Dr. S. didn't get to teach what he's learned about elbows to you guys, but Dr. H. told me you've done some. I want you to do Mac's. I'll assume the risk; it'll be on me, not you. I'll sign a release if you like. So my question is will you?"

He hesitated, and I could see he was looking for the right words before answering.

"I'd be guessing, and hoping that what I think might work will help," he said, and fell silent. I could tell he was already thinking about it, how to approach it, and what to try. A good start, I thought.

"I'm good with that," I assured him. "The alternative is putting him down. Worst case I'll cross that one if we get there, but I'm determined not to get there and for now I'm asking – begging – that you give it a go and we see what happens. Okay?"

Dr. L. agreed and we did his right front leg first.

Incredibly, it was even more ghastly looking afterwards than the previous surgeries, but we were surgical aftercare veterans by now, quickly moved past that and into action. Given the travel time, follow-up visits were less convenient, but it was easier than roundtrips to Eugene.

The downside was Dr. L. wasn't thrilled with the results. The elbow was somewhat more stable but it was stiffer and with less range of motion than he'd hoped for. Lousy news, but as we began talking about the left elbow, he had exciting news.

"Dr. S has rallied a little down in Eugene. He hasn't recovered, but he's calling the vets in to learn about elbows."

"Wow, that's great. What does it mean for us?"

"Two things," Dr. L. said. "First, I won't do the left leg until after our time with him. And if Mac is better for it, we'll have to reassess the right elbow."

"Meaning we'll be re-doing it?" I asked, never once having considered that possibility, but open to it.

"Yes, if we see clear benefit, we will … and if we do, you'll get the family price."

"I appreciate that, I really do," I said and sighed, and stopped.

"What are you think?" Dr. L. asked me.

"There's nothing to think about. Mac is the four-legged love of my life, despite the fact he's a canine money pit, too. There is no choice for me, I have to do this. I couldn't live with myself if I didn't. We all love him so much. Everyone does. He's such a big part of our lives I can't imagine life, our house, our family, without him. We have to try and hope it works."

Later that summer when Dr. L. performed the surgery on Mac's left elbow, thanks to what he'd learned from Dr. S. it was evident that this one had in fact been more successful. The following spring, we went back in and re-did the right elbow.

And I got the family price. It was still a ton of money, but a nice discount.

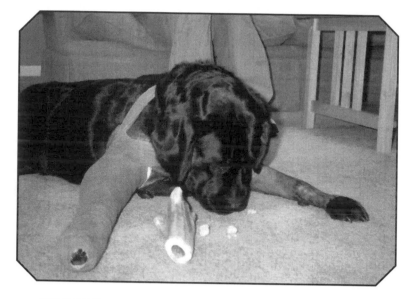

RECOVERING AFTER HIS THIRD ELBOW SURGERY.

Doing the math meant that we'd begun thinking of Mac's aggregate medical tab as his freshman and sophomore years at the University of Oregon. But as he recovered from his fifth major leg surgery, the fact was that his joyful disposition, incredibly, remained unaffected and that was its own reward.

Mac continued to amaze and delight us. His will to live and acceptance of his lot trumped everything. After five major leg surgeries he was still the happiest and most loving dog I'd ever met. Happiest of all was when he was with us.

And although he didn't fetch a ball or stick, never learned to swim and do all the things Labs are famous for loving to do, he could move better and even run a little if a squirrel ventured into his yard and he needed to kick some ass.

Paw Prints In My Heart

Our early morning walks, in all weather and usually at the crack of dark, became a fixture of our lives I cherished fiercely. Not a day passes that I don't wish we could take one more loop of the neighborhood together.

CHAPTER FOUR
Mac's wonderful Middle Years.

Living the life we'd hoped he'd have, Mac was a deliriously happy adult dog. Well-behaved, too, except one thing: a visitor protocol quirk rooted in his assumption that you were as happy to see him as he was to see you. Dog people adored him, but everyone got the uber-welcome. To me, these were charming, if socially incorrect, Mac being Mac moments, but not everyone saw it that way.

Showering you with thanks for stopping by was one thing, but nuzzling your privates was quite another. Surgeries had trumped obedience training, but I, the Obedience School dropout, devised a worthy, if fitting, workaround: Instructing visitors to how to greet him; otherwise he'd only try harder, thinking you didn't see him. Properly greeted, he'd hit the floor, and roll to his back for you to scratch his belly. It worked.

Most of my life I've been an early-riser. It's a chronic self-inflicted affliction. I joke about not having slept late since the sixties when I had good help. The early morning habit is so engrained now that, at an hour many fairly view as obscenely and incomprehensibly early, if I open one eye, my mind takes the cue and starts racing. And just like that, going back to sleep is no longer possible. The cycle only reinforces itself – I'll never change – but there's a magic in those early morning hours for me.

Starting the day in a quiet house before anyone else is awake has a privacy and an intimacy all its own. For all the years of his life, Mac shared that time with me, and we started each day together, just the two of us. To this day I'm still surprised how many mornings I'm still surprised that he's no longer around and I have to begin the day alone.

We had a routine, established and repeated all his life. Every morning, first order of business before the coffee and newspaper I can't function without, I'd make a beeline for Mac's kennel to let him out if he hadn't already let himself out. For most of his life, his kennel was where he started and ended his day. He truly loved it, and outgrew two before settling into the XXL size. The kennel was his space; cozy and safe, and comfy with a nice nest of old comforters he liked to rip apart and pull the ticking out before burrowing down deeply into them and going to sleep. I never bothered locking it. Mac never objected to going in.

In fact, it quickly became his preference, at the end of the day, what came to be known in our family as *beddy time*. Baby talk in falsetto from my boys and me, our Mackie voices. We're big guys, and I know it seems so silly, but I'm smiling as I remember it. Talking to him using our Mackie voices seemed so natural.

Like anything Mac did more than once, his routine for beddy time became an instant ritual. It was the one time of day he had little patience and was all business, demanding an escort and quick service. As the evening wore on he'd move from favorite spots at our feet to ones farther across the room, positioned halfway between us and the kennel. Then, when it was time, out of nowhere, and usually after briefly napping, he'd boom a bark or two; making it official and letting us know it was beddy time.

"Ready for beddy?" I'd ask, and he gave me a look that said, "C'mon, get a move-on." As I stood, he'd already have turned and would be on his way. He'd drop anything – other than food – anytime, for attention and a scratch or a pet, but this was the one time of day he wasn't at all interested in anything but hitting the sack. Opening the door to the kennel, he'd go in without the slightest hesitation. I countered this with a ritual of my own, starting my hand on his head and running down his spine to his tail as he disappeared inside, as my way of saying good night.

As the years passed, most mornings he'd be out of his kennel when I appeared in the family room, and we'd greet each other enthusiastically. On those occasions when he slept in, it was a little more of a party. He'd explode out the door when I opened it, celebrating like long-lost pals reunited, wriggling joyfully, spinning in tight circles around my feet, often getting tangled-up and nearly sending me toppling down onto him. Stopping, he'd transfer his energy to his celebrated feverish kisses delivered to whatever body part or article of clothing was within reach of his massive tongue.

Breakfast wasn't a Ho Hum-everyday-going-through-the-motions thing. It was a big event, joyous even. You'd think we'd starved him and it had been days since his last meal. He was always hungry, and he was a big boy. A big boy that got little exercise. Weight management entered the picture with strict portions of the lowest fat food I could buy. Only available through the vet, of course, and priced to prove it, which I'm sure shocks no one.

Anyway, what he was fed didn't seem enough but with his surgically repaired joints, maintaining his weight or taking off a few pounds beat packing more on. These things combined to make each meal, the real highpoints of the day. Doing it justice, Mac attacked his breakfast and dinner with gusto and a workmanlike approach. Total concentration and focus. Head down in his bowl, he didn't look up until it was case closed, chowing away without ever taking a breath and not reappearing until the bowl was licked clean and no trace of anything at all remained. Mac had a similarly single-minded focused approach to his water bowl, often draining a good-sized bowl completely and then rushing over to thrust his huge dripping muzzle in our faces to say thanks.

After breakfast, I'd let him out. It would give me time for a cup of coffee and maybe the paper or at least a quick peek at it, because letting him out was only buying time for the other truly great daily event in his life – our morning walk. Mac was only willing to wait quietly so long. I think he felt I was entitled to a little time, and this was his way of setting a time limit. I appreciated the consideration, but the countdown was on.

He only had so much patience, and if pushed beyond his limits he wasn't bashful about pushing back. Eyes trained on me; moving, flinching, reacting with my every move, he was willing to wait – but not indefinitely – and actually not very long at all. Breakfast and a casual trip to the back yard were no substitute for the morning walk; his favorite part of the day.

After eating, he'd settle down either at my feet, or a short distance away, licking his chops and cleaning up. He would be briefly peaceful and laying on his stomach, invariably with his front paws crossed, as he'd always done. It must be the breed's classic pose because once on vacation we saw it rendered in a pair of stone Labs adorning the entry to gardens outside of a hotel in Hawaii. That habit of his charmed us when he was a pup, and we feared, briefly, that all the hardware in his joints after five surgeries might be the end of it, but it endured.

The clock was ticking, it was time for a *walkie*.

I'd get up, pick up the leash hanging in the mudroom and he'd essentially go bonkers. Jumping, spinning, chasing his tail, and not making it easy to attach his leash. Then he'd drag me down the street, sometimes running a little, a very short distance, with his lead in his mouth and at that moment I felt there was no happier dog on earth.

Most days it was just the two of us, possibly with a few other hearty souls out and about so early, and the newspaper delivery folk. Most people, runners or dog walkers, didn't get started as early as we did. The two of us had amazing albeit one-sided conversations on those solitary daily jaunts as I made Mac privy to all my secrets. He was a great listener.

In winter it was dark and rainy; in summer we'd see many sunrises, and I enjoyed the private showings we shared. I'd talk to him as we retraced again the same routes we had covered before, over and over again, the same routes he never tired of or grew bored with, sniffing the very things he'd sniffed most every day with unrestrained fascination like they were brand new. Other than the few times when for medical reasons walks weren't allowed, healthy or sick, I walked him every day, rain or shine.

The week's biggest outing was the Sunday walk to a coffee shop not far from us where year 'round Lynne and I sat outside and had coffee, with Mac contentedly holding court at our feet. When you do something like that for years at a neighborhood haunt like that you can't help but become a kind of community fixture. Mac, more than us, I couldn't help but think. It was amazing to watch people's reactions. He was a dog that made eye contact with you; he was never submissive that way. Dog people took to him immediately, and couldn't pass by without stopping or at least saying something to him as they passed by.

But strangers I expected nothing from surprised me. Folks who by their look had little interest in socializing with anyone on a Sunday morning, and certainly not a strange dog. But as they passed, he'd make eye contact with each of them. And unfailingly, frowns became smiles. Instead of walking by, they'd slow and say something to him, or ask to pet him. Many stopped and visited with us, and because of Mac, became friends. One woman in her eighties became a regular, seeking him out each Sunday before joining her friends inside. As the years passed, more and more, without talking about it, we were all celebrating him still being around.

Our dogs love us and accept us. I'd often joke "in spite of myself," but I've come to appreciate that such unconditional affection is in large measure what deepens the bonds. In Mac's case, it went a bit further. I think of it as the product of what he felt and the fact that we spent so much time together.

He bathed all of us with a purity of affection from soulful adoring eyes, warm and dark and twinkling brightly. But

I swear it was more than affection he was conveying his gratitude for all we'd done, and his utter delight for his life and happiness being with us. I know it may sound far-fetched, but every one of us believes that Mac knew he was a truly lucky guy and that, in his way, he was grateful to be around and to be with us.

We felt lucky, too. That's quite a statement when we tallied the uncertainty, fears, work and dollars that had constituted his first three years, but it had all been worth it. And it was gratifying that he was letting us know he knew and appreciated it. Whether this is a dog lover reading more into a four-legged friend's expression than could possibly be there or what I'd rather believe, there was no doubt that Mac had inarguably landed in the right house.

In our house, the Mutual Admiration Society met daily.

We were all nuts about him but he and I spent an unbelievable amount of time together. I was the first to greet him in the morning and the last face he saw at night. I'd left the corporate life and was working from home; consulting, developing and hustling a reality show for sports fans I never sold, before ultimately transitioning into what became my future: heeding the call to write. Our kids were in high school, at college or on their own, and Lynne was often out much of the day. I was usually around, and had more time with Mac than anyone else.

Fitting, because while he loved us all, I was his best bud, and I guess you could say his dad. Somehow I can't think of myself as his master, although I suppose I certainly was, but that doesn't do justice to the remarkable friendship that evolved between the two of us. When I traveled and was away, even on short trips, I missed him, and asked about him when I called home. I tried to ask about the kids first, and I think I did. Lynne invariably remarked that when I was away, he looked around for me, clearly missed me, and was a bit subdued and not quite himself.

For the rest of his life, this would be his response to my occasional absence.

Funny thing, the rest of family got along without me just fine.

Our daughter, Meagan, gave me a real gift when Mac was around four. She hadn't yet moved to the Bay Area, still living and working in Portland, and she came over to the house for dinner one night. In hand was the first digital camera I'd ever seen. She took a few shots of Mac "helping" Lynne cook our dinner. From his wisely-selected central spot in our not overlarge kitchen, he situated himself smack-dab in the thick of the action. Ready for treats Lynne might give him or whatever hit the floor along the way. Those hardwood floors weren't easy for him to navigate, but radiant heat made them delightfully warm and more than worth the inconvenience, comforting his artificially enhanced joints and bones that surely felt older than their chronology.

Meagan took a shot that night I've come to name the Portrait, one of my all-time favorite pictures, and the more I think about, maybe the classic Mac pic. I loved it then but treasure it now. Ever more appreciative of it because I realize now that in those years as a culture we were between photo generations. For us, video mostly killed taking pictures. We do have some, and a few are classics, but the Portrait is my desktop background to this day and may always be. A framed

8 x 10 is on a table just inside our family room, just off the kitchen, where Mac lived and spent most of his time. Sliding doors by his kennel opened to the back yard.

As luck had it, he couldn't have been posed better: handsome, but serious and mature, older and more stately-looking than his years. There is slight greying around his muzzle, so striking against the black, although in human years he was barely thirty. Early gray meant something, didn't it? I suspected a byproduct of surgeries, going under so often, and not just genetics. I never talked about it with the family, or asked the vet, but I knew he was older than his years. I instead made light of him going grey early like me; he got it from his *dad*. My first grey hair arrived in my early teens, so looking at Mac I felt solidarity with him because of it. In truth, thus far, he'd aged far better than I; getting better looking as I just got older looking.

I also remember feeling a tug at my heart, the greying muzzle triggering the faintest emotional chill I knew was about the future. Inevitable, and I accepted it, of course, but it heralded an accelerating future I dreaded. In those years, and considering he was a bionic Lab, he was enjoying comparatively good health. All things considered, he got around pretty well for the non-athlete he'd always be, living a pretty normal and a definitely happy dog's life. All of which thrilled us because it was what we'd hoped for: an acceptable quality of life.

The basis for my considerations and concerns came from riding the medical point. All of the logistics, discussions with surgeons, transporting him back and forth, coordinating, managing recuperations, and medications, and all the basics of

MAC'S PORTRAIT PIC.

day-to-day TLC with an ever-watchful eye. Looking for what, I was never certain, but looking for it nonetheless. The aggregate physical toll on his body was unknown. It could be not much or quite a lot. Either way the currency, when settlement day arrived, would be measured in years. To me, the early grey was evidence it was closer and coming sooner than I cared to think about.

Not the cheeriest of thoughts for a head-over-heels dog owner, but I lived with it and kept it to myself, resolving to enjoy his time to the fullest. For years I had believed that early on in the process one of the docs had said something about "eight years" but I never confirmed that he had. Or I decided I'd invented it as a self-defense mechanism to steel myself ahead of time against the unknown future, perhaps subconsciously laying a foundation of mental insulation.

As if that were possible.

Even if the years weren't shortened, I saw 'equipment failure' as logically predictable. There would be years of mechanical wear and tear, exacerbated by occasional bursts of activity, or bad luck, and I confess I'd become a little fixated on getting a handle on his effective age.

Mac was now in his human thirties by my calculations, and a handsome devil in his prime. I'd always heard that a dog year equals seven human years but learned that's not exactly so; seven years is how it averages over the first ten years. It starts quickly. A dog reaches puberty in the first year, so call it sixteen years. The second year is eight, the third is six, and for each year thereafter, five human years for each dog year.

For the next five years or so, until he was eight, other than the physical limitations we'd adjusted to somewhat, and that he was oblivious and indifferent to, we were all one big happy family. While "Dad loves Mac best" had indeed become a family joke, the truth is that while I may have set the pace, I wasn't the only one. Everyone in the family had simply gone gaga over this dog, and loved him best. He had a complex relationship with each of us.

That kind of interaction wasn't limited to just the family, but something he extended to mostly all the people in his life. I think that explains why virtually everyone that met him loved him; when a dog loves you, and Mac made it clear he did, it's hard not to love back. He became known for his greetings. A new arrival was an event, a genuinely fascinating and wonderful new friend – immediately one of his favorites – and, as was his way, received his undivided attention. Shaking and wriggling, beaming joyful, soulful eyes, and demonstrating how thrilled he was with unrestrained doggie kisses delivered by an impressive tongue that meant business. I learned to live with the fact that my technique at the door, while a bit unconventional and somewhat of a personal embarrassment was *awkward*, but it calmed him and was the best I could do.

When Mac first met you, he treated you like a long lost friend.

When Mac knew you, he greeted you like his very best friend.

Mac had many friendships outside the family. Our sons' friends loved him and over the years this was manifested in interesting ways. When our boys were off to college and we'd run into some of their high school friends who were still in town, after brief conversations catching up with Lynne and me came the predictable question:

"*How's Mac?*"

"He's a happy guy," I'd answer, warmed by the thought of how true that was, and at how happy we all were having him around.

"I'm sure he'd love to see you if you're ever in the neighborhood," I sometimes added.

A few of the kids took me up on it. Mac would celebrate their arrival by tearing around the pool table, running laps until panting and out of breath, before turning his full attention to properly expressing his thanks for thinking of him and stopping by. If these guests appeared in the family room, they were subject to the same front door greeting requirements. Greet him, reach out a hand which sent him to his back, his massive belly offered up for requisite scratching they'd been trained to deliver.

"How's Mac?" would later take on special meaning for us. Our middle son, a Captain and combat engineer with the 82nd Airborne in Iraq and Afghanistan, was away for many of those years, and stationed at Ft. Bragg in North Carolina between deployments. Calls came regularly irregularly, so Lynne and I anxiously awaited them. Before we chatted about his life in the war zone or North Carolina, or ours on the home front, Evan would invariably and without exception first ask what would become his trademark opening to every call:

"How's Mac?"

Happily, for much of the time, I could answer "He's fine." and say it truthfully. With five leg surgeries in the rear-view mirror, we'd settled into a normal, everyday life. Mac was a, maybe the, fixture at the heart of it. He couldn't have been happier because he got what he wanted more than anything which was to be with us. And we had him, and couldn't have been happier for it.

To Evan, I might have added, "And he's getting his twenty hours of sleep, too," because as he grew older, it seemed that while he was usually with us, he was often napping and snoring. As he grew older, he refined his snoring technique, featuring a deep doggie baritone that rumbled impressively, and which became part of our family soundtrack. I'm assured, however, that as good as he was, his snoring was never a match for mine, and that on more than one occasion the two of us treated the family to snoring duets that emptied the room. I can't count the times a number of us began watching something on television, and a few hours later I'd awaken, alone.

Alone in an empty family room with Mac snoozing away. Thank God for DVRs.

On nice days he had his favorite spots in the yard, and spent a fair amount of time there. Some days he'd take naps in the shade, but as he grew older found the hot sun to warm his bones. The yard was just about perfect for a city dog and a house dog at that. If we were outside, he'd join us, but if we came in, he'd soon follow. He was always a people-first dog. Mac liked other dogs well enough, but loved and preferred people. He just wanted to be with us wherever we were, whatever we were doing.

Everywhere, that is, but in the car. Over all the years with all the requisite car trips to vets, or short outings we tried to make work out, Mac just never ever became a car dog. All those heartwarming family scenes in commercials with dogs along for the ride going to the mountains, the beach, on errands, wherever, all of those classic dog moments had nothing to do with us. Which was no big deal; we simply added that to the list of stuff he'd never or do and didn't care to do.

We assumed the problem with cars was he just couldn't get comfortable. For whatever reason he didn't lie down instead he stood all the while. Add to this the fact that his legs weren't strong enough to stand like that for extended periods. Although he enjoyed hanging his head out the window in the wind, it was clear that long drives were out of the question. He was mostly indifferent to short ones, and would much rather not go at all, being more than happy to be left behind when we went out. It just made him all the more thrilled to see us when we returned and all the more eager to make up for lost time when we did.

A great fan of hanging out with us as the years passed, he found a number of evolving favorite resting spots around the house. The absolute favorite of all may have been outside on the patio in front of the sliding doors. To give him easy access in and out without needing supervision during nice weather, I persuaded a local screen company to build a custom sliding screen with a built-in doggie exit for the sliding door. This was unquestionably the engineering highpoint of my life. It's still in place, and to me, a proud testament to my totally accidental engineering crowning achievement. I will always be amazed they didn't sell a ton of them.

Another choice spot was at our feet watching television in the family room; one half of his body in the family room, and sprawled across the threshold, half in the kitchen. I took it as his way of being in both places at once. He loved the floor, ensconced against the wall in a corner of the kitchen. Literally loved it, licking it as he lay on his back, legs stretched out fully in front and behind of his body Snoopy-style. Why the wall? I always assumed it was simply because it was there and within reach, and as one of the great lickers that I'll ever know, good enough reason for Mac.

Mac was no longer a dumb-ass puppy, but now a mature dog, wise to the ways of the world and finely-tuned to the inner workings of his family. Politely he had learned how to manipulate us to get what he wanted and over the years became increasingly skilled making it happen. I didn't mind; I admired that. I think we all did.

Meal time is one of the great examples of this, maybe the very best.

In fact, breakfast and dinner, in their ways, were daily marquee events.

Because I started the day early, we started the day early, so breakfast was early.

Mac was always ready, devoured his meal with gusto and purpose, and I often felt badly that it seemed such a modest portion and not enough, by any measure, to give him enough to make it to dinner. Made all the more difficult thanks to my chronic affliction as an early-riser. Regrettably, I couldn't do anything to change it. The afternoons were long waits for dinner.

As a result, dinner became a priority not long after the euphoria of breakfast faded. Difficult, and before long impossible, to wait until it was near time for our dinner, Mac had his own schedule. He was hungry, always, but as the afternoon wore on this morphed into a blend of antsy and ravenous. We learned to avoid saying the word 'dinner' and took to spelling it out, along with other key words he understood that elicited responses we wanted to avoid if we could. His vocabulary was so impressive, that as he grew older we spelled a lot.

It wasn't long before dinner had moved five-thirty to five o'clock, then to four o'clock, and then in later years to three and then closer to two. Whatever the time du jour was, Mac would be set-up in position to work us in an attempt to move the time for dinner still farther forward. He was winning this one, but there were benefits. A full belly calmed him, and he never begged while we ate hours later, but he never stopped pushing for earlier.

It was our own family game show: *How Early Can You Eat?*

Playing to win, Mac was winning and had a clock in his stomach that truly performed like clockwork. Like a baseball player that gets to the ballpark early to prepare and get ready, when it was dinnertime he'd have already been sitting in front of us and watching our every move. Eyes riveted, anticipating and responding to our every movement that might signal it was time. Willing us on, and as the years passed, pushing the time envelope forward. The cause and effect was clear: The earlier he ate breakfast, the earlier he'd go on dinner alert. We'd moved steadily in the wrong direction and couldn't go back. Mac clearly understood the power of bugging us, and he'd win because we'd give in. He'd wear us down, adjusting the internal clock in his stomach. At the end of his life it was even earlier.

But back to his astounding vocabulary.

A smart guy, he understood stuff, learned to anticipate many things, and wisely knew when it was in his best interests to disappear or when to be around. But I don't think anything impressed me more than his vocabulary; a lot of words, from people's names to things. He heard them and reacted appropriately. I thought that was really cool. What I didn't expect was that he understood simple sentences; but it didn't end there.

We began giving him complex instructions which he'd follow, because he understood.

During nice weather, Lynne loves nothing more than passing time in the afternoon on the deck off our bedroom, on a chaise lounge with a good book. She likes it enough to give it a go in not so nice weather, bundling up in sweatshirts and under blankets, taking full advantage of any opportunity to be outside. Before long, Mac joined her at every opportunity, able to get up on the deck from the yard, and even found his own place there, next to an ideally positioned brick planter. The planter's top rose just above the deck at the perfect height for a headrest for the massive head that was always looking for a resting spot with support and this one was perfect. It even came with a great view over the yard. Sometimes Lynne would be on her deck without Mac knowing it.

Just for fun, I thought I'd tell him and see what he did.

"Mac, go see Mommy on her deck," I'd tell him.

He gave me a brief glance. No confusion in his eyes, he understood perfectly.

The glance was so matter of fact, I almost expected him to nod in agreement.

He got up, went out the doggie-door, through the yard and joined her on the deck.

We tested him a few times to be sure this wasn't a bizarre coincidence. In a way we were like proud parents, because this was a momentous event. We talked about it a lot, always thrilled by it. It only further reflected what I was coming to understand wasn't a gaga pet owner's delusion, but evidence of a relationship more complex than I ever thought possible. This also cast a different light upon our conversations, albeit one-sided ones, on our walks.

He listened and understood a lot.

Before long I tested another sentence. Like the first, it had instructions.

On weekend summer evenings, and in late spring or early fall as the weather allows, Lynne and I enjoy a drink together on the big patio, sitting and talking as we listen to music. In Oregon we take advantage of good weather without hesitation. This patio is at the opposite end of the house. This sentence and instructions were a bit more complicated. The distance is greater, and it features a key word we used much less frequently. In the family room I gave Mac his marching orders and half-expected him to look at me with a blank stare.

"Meet us on the patio, Mackie," I told him, and repeated it.

To test him, I went to the patio through the kitchen, closing the door behind me. Mac would be left behind with no one to repeat or reinforce the message. For him to pull this off he'd have to go out the doggie door, across the yard and around the house, and up a short flight of steps to the patio. Even if he did understand, leaving him abruptly behind the closed door I'd disappeared through might easily be more than enough to confuse and distract him.

Right?

"Meet us on the patio, Mackie," I repeated.

As I turned to leave, he rose from the floor and walked the opposite way to doggie door. Mac had paid no attention to what I was doing, but remained focused on what he was doing. As a result, he was there waiting for us when we arrived, facing the door we'd walked through, sitting there with his tail wagging and a smile on his face.

That he knew lots of words, names, things, and could connect them was a lot of fun.

Lynne used his knowledge of others skillfully.

If Mac was bugging her, more often than not around his dinnertime, or later when she'd be preparing ours, she discovered a handy-dandy way to get him out of her hair and into mine.

All she had to do was say, "Mac, go see your *father!*"

And he'd get up to find me. Countless times at work in my office I'd look up to see he'd joined me. Another thing I miss about him.

Paw Prints In My Heart

So many things became habits, and like most dogs Mac was a sweet creature of habit. Little things, insignificant things, silly habits, are memories now, but what matters now is holding on to them to prevent them from fading. I still hear the clicking of his nails on the floors, the tinkling of the silver chain collar he wore for many years, the way he yawned, and how in the first minutes of countless early mornings as I picked up his bowl and walked to where we kept his food to fill it for his breakfast, he followed me, and snorted. Every time and without fail, I took the snort as something akin to approval and his way of offering encouragement and urging me on.

His devotion and dedication to taking a walk rivaled, or surpassed, the US Postal Service.

Sometimes in snow and on icy streets so crippling the city was literally shut down, when the daily walk was still happening, stepping outside the door on those days was nothing less than a dangerous undertaking. Even on slight hills, an icy misstep was a real risk. But the walk was everything to him, and in many ways it was everything to me, as well. It was also our time, our special time together, outdoors in the world, just the two of us.

Leash in his mouth dragging me down the street, ignoring whatever pain it might give him before thinking better of it, and me fighting to slow him down for both of our safety. Mac often limping home because of it; deliberate, though gimpy, the price paid for that small window of time when he was being a dog and doing what most dogs do instinctively and routinely. Things that he never could without carefully monitored, controlled, and supervised conditions with his dad and best friend watching closely.

Those walks mattered so much to us both, and as a treat on special occasions, when he was doing well or on a particularly beautiful later afternoon or evening, I'd occasionally add a bonus walk; a short nighttime jaunt around the neighborhood. Less frequently as the years passed, and usually prompted by my loose tongue uttering the word *walk*. Once said, there was no pulling it back.

But we learned.

"Have you taken Mac for his W-A-L-K?" Lynne asked each morning when she joined us in the family room.

Spelling it out was no longer optional.

Mackie was a smart boy.

THE PLANTER WAS A PERFECT HEAD-REST.

CHAPTER FIVE
At Eight Years Old Big Trouble Finds Us

At eight the next medical crisis was only a matter of time. I'd always held 'eight' in my head as a moment of truth age, a medical milestone. When trouble came, while it was not unexpected, it still hit hard. Knowing what's coming makes it no less unnerving.

Mac had been doing well, orthopedically-adjusted, with no real major issues. But no longer. Out for our walk per usual one morning, nearing home he was limping badly, as if his joints had seized up, refusing to do what was asked of them. Barely able to hobble, and so helpless it broke my heart, scared, I almost carried him home.

The day had begun like so many others.

Entering the family room around 5 a.m., I found Mac had let himself out of the kennel, was waiting for me and ready for breakfast. Happy, ready for day. Wriggling and spinning in circles he sought out my hand and gave it feverish kisses. For me, it was my daily reinforcement that in his eyes I was perfect.

A sentiment that I returned, guilty as charged; like Lynne told me so often, "For you, Mac can do no wrong."

I couldn't argue – I'd forgive him anything.

So that morning after struggling home, after he'd hobbled sadly inside, and I'd put my panic aside, I got to work on what to do about it. I was unnerved; certain something was up and I had no doubt that something wasn't good. There was also no doubt that I had to get on it and right away.

"What's wrong?" Lynne asked. She had a sixth sense with this, she felt it.

Sitting with a steaming cup of coffee and the morning paper, watching Good Morning America, she'd heard something in my tone talking to Mac coming in through the mudroom. Or maybe she just caught the vibe. No surprise; I was rattled. Like so many times throughout his life, while she didn't quite precisely say it, she often scolded me for my tendency to panic, see the worst and overreact. I don't get up each day looking for trouble and take no pleasure in finding gloom and doom, and I *do* overreact at times. Sometimes for the right reasons and sometimes not so much, but this time there was none of that. She sensed it, too. After all we'd been through, what we knew and all we feared because of it, it appeared likely to me that real medical trouble had found us again. We both felt it and I struggled briefly, organizing my thoughts so I could put them into words.

Mac limped slowly to her as I quickly related how our morning walk had gone south. He seemed physically diminished, somewhat unstable, and watching his sad, hobbled half-steps, she listened to me with a pained look on her face.

"I see what you mean," she began. "This is different; I've never seen him quite like this. What are we going to do?" she asked.

"Call the vet, tell her what's up and see what she thinks," I answered without hesitation, but sighed deeply before continuing.

"As you know, that phone call is always the first step, though rarely the last," I added with a forced smile. "I take it you can see that I'm not crying wolf, and that this time something's up?"

She nodded, she did. "And you'll do ... what?"

"Whatever we can, whatever it takes; that's what Mackie gets. Right, baby boy?" At the sound of my voice and knowing I was speaking to him, he walked over to me.

By all appearances he had partially recovered, I thought, limping less and showing no lasting ill effects. This was so typical and true to character. Ever the ultimate stoic accepting whatever is, in any and all circumstances, adjusting, accepting and compensating. He was not at all distressed in the slightest that minutes earlier he'd been virtually crippled and unable to move.

For now, he'd quickly rebounded. But while I was thrilled to see him back to his usual self, I couldn't shake the image from my mind. This time I wouldn't rationalize it away, or persuade myself it could wait a while because he was rallying. As tempting as it was to believe it was an anomaly, I knew better. I had no doubt the time had come to get proactive and do something.

Still, for the moment, the difference in Mac was remarkable.

That dog had been virtually unable to walk, crippled, incapable and hobbling. The smile on his face was almost a tad apologetic for causing all the upset and inconvenience. Now at home, this was sharply contrasted by a miraculous and instantaneous recovery, like it never happened and all was well.

His way of saying, "Relax. No biggie, pops; all is good."

On other occasions Lynne might have said that, too. Every time our fragile status-quo was disrupted, it didn't automatically translate to crisis, and that's fair. Also fair was to evaluate each event because when crisis came, we had to act. We thought of Mac as the ultimate survivor, a dog that adapted, hell, embraced whatever came along because that's all he knew; he lived with a good-natured acceptance of his normal as he had all his life. My problem was this time I couldn't.

The alarm was screaming in my head.

Nothing would have made me happier than a non-event. But I had no doubt that this was anything but a non-event.

My vivid memories of the bad old days, the surgeries, came rushing back.

We were back in *what-the-hell-do-we-do-now* mode and I hated returning to it. With a deep sigh, slowly shaking my head and quietly groaning at the thought of all that went into gathering options, assessing them, and then figuring out a plan, wondering if it would work, or even made sense, we plunged forth with a hope and a prayer.

Bearing in mind, too, that Mac was no puppy now; more of his life was behind him than lay ahead. If surgery was needed, would we do it? Even if we did, could he survive it?

My guess is that he would, but even so, did that make sense on the quality of life scale? And if it didn't make sense, and it became *hard choices time*, could I be sensible?

Could I make the hard call?

I thought about that a lot. And wondered.

I tried never to think about it in terms of money and was nominally successful. Sticker shock at the vet is hard to avoid, but in truth it was never about the money; always it was what we could or couldn't do, and could or couldn't expect. I can't count how many people over the years asked us if we'd considered pet medical insurance. If only.

The forty thousand dollar rhetorical question.

Given Mac's hefty medical tab, any relief would have been more than welcomed. Pet insurance like all insurance is a two-edged sword painfully cutting both ways. We didn't have it then and too bad for us, and if you don't get it before, you'll never get it after. My consolation was knowing that even if we'd had it, if pet insurance functions anything like people insurance, they would have cancelled his doggie butt after the first surgery.

Whether we were facing a hiccup along the medical trail, or the big wake-up call and jump-start to whatever came next, I needed direction to do whatever it would be that needed doing. Once again sorting through shitty options to find something that hopefully worked.

Whatever my concerns, Mac was happily oblivious. Settled inside, he lay down and got right to work on a nap. Dogs sleep a lot, and Mac was no exception. I'd long joked that "Mac just isn't himself without his 20 hours of sleep a day." I watched him sleeping peacefully, snoring deeper than ever in that rumbling way of his, almost feeling the vibrations across the room, and reached for the phone.

"Tell me what's happening," Dr. E. said gently, returning my call sooner than I'd expected despite her Tuesday mornings filled with surgeries. While waiting I'd had ample time to craft a scenario that told the story as succinctly as a worried wordsmith was capable of doing.

"Are you giving him Rimadyl daily?" she asked after hearing it.

Rimadyl is the doggie arthritis anti-inflammatory med of choice from Pfizer.

"No, only when he needs it, and lately that hasn't been often," I answered, wondering if I'd been remiss, kicking myself if I had been, and then wondering if it would have mattered.

"Let's make it every day, 100mg, twice a day for the next week, then just once a day and we'll see if it helps. My guess is he needs it."

"And what else?" I asked, knowing there was more.

"I think Dr. H. should take a look him; he hasn't really seen him since he did those first surgeries. Mac's eight now – seven years since the hind legs and hips – maybe he'll have ideas about other things we can do. I'll call him, tell him the story and what we're doing and to expect your call."

"Is he still at the referral clinic?"

Dr. E's smile came through the phone when she answered.

"No, he's moved up in the world, has his own clinic now. You'll be impressed."

And I was.

Two days later Mac and I made our first visit to the Mt.

Cascadia Referral Clinic.

There was every reason to be impressed.

The facility was beautifully designed, a high-tech medical center with clean modern lines, stone, wood and glass that was so Oregon and, I guessed, expensive. The building looked like it belonged there, and was also beautifully situated. A remarkably peaceful almost tranquil, spot given its freeway access, in the heart of the city and only minutes from downtown. Just off Pacific Highway in Southwest Portland, down a small hill and set back a little from the steady traffic. As a piece of real estate the land was a gem in every sense.

Hold on to your wallet time, I realized and laughed at the thought.

This was Mac.

And Mac, by the way, was thrilled.

To him, yet another trip to the vet, even a new one, meant new friends not old traumas. He loved going to the vet even if it was by car which he accepted stoically and good naturedly. For the past five years we'd hardly been strangers at the vet, but I sensed that now we were on the threshold of becoming regulars again. No shivering, shaking, no anxiety; he wasn't nervous. He was right in his element and actually couldn't have been happier. Delighted to be the medical center of attention, he greeted and charmed everyone we saw before Dr. H. came out to see us.

After greeting each other like old soldiers, and the more I thought about it did seem fitting the three of us had certainly been to battle together, he said, "I came out because before I examine him inside I'd like to see him walk around outside."

And he did that, putting Mac through his paces

comprehensively and efficiently; from close and far, coming and going and there was no question he knew exactly what he was looking for. He asked me a few questions along the way, and I jumped in with a few of mine as he was wrapping up and we prepared to go inside for the more formal examination.

"He's been better with Rimadyl twice a day but he's also slower and stiffer … so let me ask you this: If he needed surgery could he survive it?" True to form, I'd wasted no time asking the *big* question.

"Sure, he's healthy, almost hearty, in his way," Dr. H. answered. "Yes, I'd say he should."

"Okay, but does he need it? And before you answer I'll ask still another one … what I asked you seven years ago – the quality of life question."

"I'm not thinking surgery. Not now, maybe not ever; there are other therapies to try first. Adequan injections have helped a lot of dogs. Some people call it a miracle drug for canine arthritis and a wonder drug for joint problems."

He told me about it and what we'd do.

Adequan, it turned out, was a remarkable drug originally developed for horses. Vets had been experimenting with hyaluronic acid injected into horse's arthritic joints to lubricate them since the seventies. After trying lots of things they'd found Adequan worked best and its usage had become widespread and common. Most critically, they had seen equal success, defined by absorption into the bloodstream and reaching the critical areas of joints, when injected into muscle, and this was what proved to be the big game-changer. It wasn't long before treatment for dogs, and then cats, followed. Adequan became the drug of choice for arthritic dogs and dogs that had major joint issues like Mac. Hope was beginning to flicker in me.

This was the first good news and we surely needed some good news.

It got better, too.

There were solid clinical indications that Adequan could prevent further cartilage loss, and in some cases even repair damage. I had no illusions we'd be that lucky; Mac's joints were way too far gone. But if it could relieve bone-on-bone, the chief source of his pain, well, that was simply huge. Mac had virtually no cartilage in his elbows, his front legs, so it couldn't protect or heal cartilage he didn't have. Fine, but lubricating his joints and making the most of what cartilage he did have made it more than worth giving Adequan a real shot. The fact was at that moment I'd have given practically anything a shot.

Looking back, I couldn't have known then how I'd prove it in the years ahead.

Online I found dog owner forums and read post after post from owners singing the praises of Adequan with stories about their dogs becoming more playful and active than they'd been in years; for some, it was like a second puppyhood. That sounded particularly good to me, because Mac had been cheated out of much of his puppyhood. Any chance for him now, to get around better and do it with less pain, seemed like a more than fair bargain and welcome news for a guy that a couple of days earlier could barely get around at all.

In his low key manner, Dr. H. had been enthusiastic and optimistic, giving me real hope that this was a solid shot at getting the help I was looking for which I had all but given up believing existed. And this was no supplement but a serious drug coming to us, in turned out, with the added muscle that the FDA had approved in 1997.

The manufacturer's website says:

Numerous studies show that Adequan® Canine (polysulfated glycosaminoglycan) can slow the cartilage from breaking down and actually supports the repair process. And unlike nutritional supplements, Adequan® Canine is FDA-approved* so you can be assured of its effectiveness.

That sure sounded good. Imagine actually getting what we were about to pay for.

Of course it also meant really paying for what we would get.

Dr. H. asked me if I was comfortable giving Mac injections.

And I wasn't once I found out what it meant.

Under the skin, I could have. But this was into the muscle; I didn't think so.

Although there would be many shots, especially in the first three months, and the drug wasn't inexpensive, I'd have my regular vet do it, and I would look for the cheapest source. The price my vet quoted put me on the hunt for an alternative right away. The irony is I could buy Adequan cheaper from pet pharmacies than my vet could from the manufacturer. It made no sense to me but health care – for dogs or people – never had made sense. Veterinary drugs and services suffer from many of the same inexplicable afflictions of people drugs and medical services.

Whatever. We'd play the hand we'd been dealt and I was happy to have a hand to play.

Adequan therapy commenced with a progression of shots

that started with injections twice a week for two weeks. This then changed to once a week for two weeks, followed by shots every other week for four weeks, and then every third week for six weeks, before finally settling into a monthly groove which I made every four weeks.

Those monthly visits became Mac's medical lifestyle for the rest of his life.

Many trips to the vet meant frequency ramping up. It meant lots of in and out of the car. Never a car dog but always accepting about it, now the logistics were completely up to me. In his youth, at his physically-adjusted best, he'd hopped up and in the car mostly well enough. No longer. Those days were gone and I was looking at the realities of age and mechanically-repaired joints catching up with us.

Mac no longer leaped into the car on his own, but now needed an assist. Always truly a heavy hunk 'o dog, I was doing more assisting than ever because he needed it more than ever. But I was getting older, too. Eventually I'd nominally master the art of getting him in and out of the car without throwing out my back or blowing it. More than once I lost control of my awkward load and curse if he spilled and tumbled out the last part of the way, jarring those fragile joints and giving me even more to worry over and feel guilty about.

Whatever the hassle, these drugs quickly became staples for us. My job was to make sure we would never run out of them. Simple enough, but I'd learn over the years it wouldn't be easy. My vet didn't inspire confidence in the world of online pet pharmacies, but with my fair share of reservations and well-intended advice, all I could do was to keep my eyes wide open.

"Yes, you can save money, but, no, you don't always know what you're getting."

This was my introduction to the sketchy world of online pet pharmacies.

It's big business, and there are lots of players. Like all e-stores, they can look real enough online, and as consumers it's not like we're drowning in choices for pet meds; we take what we can get and hope. I had to have Adequan and Rimadyl, and while price mattered, consistency mattered more.

Over the next five years I'd do a robust, regular business with a good number of these sites, experiencing customer service often spotty and at times shoddy. Some thrived, at least for a while, as others failed. Disappearing or morphing into another identity or brand. Sometimes the product changed, frequently departing from Novartis' original packaging and arrived without all of the consumer information I'd never actually read. But while I never ran out of either drug, at times it took extra effort, and more than once essentially starting over, finding yet another pharmacy.

Once I was shipped Adequan Equine and, dissatisfied with the vague explanation I heard when I called about it, was forced to call Novartis, Adequan's manufacturer, before my vet would inject it. It turned out to be the same product, without an added component that allowed for the canine version to be stored without being refrigerated. Adequan dosage is determined by weight. A 5ml vial for Mac represented 2-1/2 doses for him. But a horse would use multiple vials for a single dose, so for Adequan Equine storage wasn't a factor as it is for dogs.

Paw Prints In My Heart

In the end, I settled on one of the biggest and best known of the pet med pharmacies. Serious big business; I still get their catalogs which are dazzling. The pharmacy appeared to be the most professional, and unquestionably were the slickest, but that's not to say they weren't without their share of perplexing and maddening moments. My vet hinted that many of these pharmacies sold drugs that weren't directly available to them through the manufacturers; stopping just short of suggesting some black market sort of thing. In any case, Pfizer, the behemoth manufacturer of Rimadyl, didn't sell directly to the online pharmacies which meant the pharmacies got the drugs from other suppliers. That could only mean vets, I guessed, knowing there was story there, but didn't care. My only concern was whatever the workaround it worked for the online pharmacy I depended upon.

It seemed a more than reasonable enough explanation to me. I didn't care how they did it, just that they did it. We needed what we needed and I'd do whatever I had to for it. Putting up with inconvenience was how I learned the hard way that there would be issues and to plan ahead. We were just thankful for a source for Adequan and Rimadyl at a fraction of what I'd pay at my vet and the drugs were, in fact, the drugs we needed.

What mattered was that Adequan worked.

It wasn't quite a miracle, but nearly one.

Mac got along better, got up and down and moved around more freely and seemed to be generally more comfortable. The joints seizing up episode wouldn't be repeated for a few years. The years immediately ahead had new rules, rules defining our new normal; more adjustments, and more to worry about from time to time. But the fact is they were pretty good years and I'm truly grateful for them.

We took walks, occasionally longer ones, too, and Mac handled them well. He slowed at the end, but rarely limped which was great. Every so often he'd even show brief flashes of youth, running, usually exploding out the family room and sprinting after squirrels making unauthorized visits in the yard, chasing them until they scurried to safety up a tree or over the fence to a neighbor's yard.

On the other hand, what was not so good about him feeling better was Mac now felt good enough to jump a little, in his view, like a puppy, irresistible behavior and always the proper way to greet an arriving visitor.

But the biggest jumps were reserved for a private audience, whoever was feeding him.

After I filled his bowl with food in the mudroom, I'd carry it back to the refrigerator in the kitchen for his broccoli, closing the door to the kitchen from the family room behind me, keeping Mac off the slippery floors. When I returned with his food he celebrated my arrival by jumping straight in the air in total excitement like a dog in a cartoon. True story.

Broccoli. It adorned his dog food every meal for rest of his life.

With Adequan therapy underway our vet made it clear that the other component of his treatment was to get serious and find a way for him to lose weight. Mac was a big boy, dense in the way English Labs are dense, but dense even for the densest of the breed. At his peak he tipped the scales at nearly 120 pounds and Dr. F. wanted to see him closer to 95.

"Just how do we do that?" I asked her. "I almost have to

laugh. It's a wise and reasonable request that is no small feat. We don't overfeed him, we keep treats, biscuits and chewies, to a bare minimum, and give him virtually nothing from the table. He gets so little exercise because he really knows better than to run."

It turned out that broccoli was one of two things we'd do.

First, we changed to the newest lowest-fat dog food made, and, coming as absolutely no surprise, was specially formulated dog food from Purina that was only available exclusively through vets.

Paying twice the usual price for dog food just seemed our style.

Combined with almost half a pound of cooked broccoli gave him some bulk and the feeling of a full tummy with the fewest calories. For the rest of his life, the bottom shelf of our refrigerator would be home to a large casserole dish of broccoli. Large enough for a two-pound bag of frozen broccoli cuts I'd microwave. We went through it in four days or so. We always had a few bags in the freezer.

Over a period of many months, Mac dropped the weight.

He trimmed down to a rather svelte fighting weight of 95 pounds at the lowest. We'd manage to keep most of the weight he'd lost off for the rest of his life. It made a huge difference.

Even after losing all that weight, he was still the densest hunk 'o dog I'd ever known.

But he was hungry and when presented with breakfast or lunch, if possible ate with even greater passion and gusto, if that were possible, his head lowered into the bowl, not coming up for air until it was gone. With my early start to the day he had breakfast by five or five-thirty. When afternoon came he was more than a little hungry, and as the notoriously accurate clock in his stomach ticked ever louder, wanted to eat earlier and earlier.

And as was always my way, I caved and fed him, earlier and earlier.

Deservedly taking a lot of ribbing for it, but after all, he was hungry.

And he'd bug me so tirelessly and relentlessly I had no choice.

I was looking at him differently now and he looked different to me.

In two ways: His muzzle was well past a little grey, seriously going grey, but more than that was an attitude shift of sorts. Like he'd had a doggie epiphany and figured something out on some level. At first, I thought I had to be imagining it, and questioned whether dogs did stuff like this. My previous dogs hadn't, but I couldn't deny what I saw with Mac. But my life with him was different from my life with those dogs. We had more private moments, just the two us together at home, and that was part of it. There was also my ongoing role as his primary caregiver, observing him to stay in touch with his physical condition.

Much could certainly be credited to his age. He'd reached a maturity and was on the threshold of becoming an *old dog*. We had that in common.

In human years we were now contemporaries.

What impressed me was a change is his demeanor; how he carried and presented himself at times. Mac was still classically all-dog all the time in all the best ways and I'll always treasure how that never changed. Trusting, loyal, easily fooled, ridiculously enthusiastic, all the little things that make dogs so charming and endearing.

So whatever transformative thing may or may not have occurred, it wasn't at the expense of his dog-dom. At the happiest/sappiest moments his face wore that look of delirious doggie joy, dumb and sweet, devotedly smitten. Just what we'd expect from man's best friend. But there were other times when it couldn't have been more different.

I can only call it an almost cerebral or even contemplative look.

At those moments, I'd swear he was operating on a higher doggie plane if one exists; calm and relaxed, knowing and almost wise, as if he understood that his life was unusual and, as absurd as it sounds, appreciated having it. He understood how his world and life in our family worked and while there were a few mischievous things he'd never give up – such as his lifelong passion for paper products, preferably used – he was remarkably well-behaved and caused no trouble. On the other hand, we gave up paper napkins. Under the table during meals he'd snatch them away given half a chance, and roaming freely between our legs under the table he had many chances and took full advantage of them.

Remembering it brings a smile.

All of these things were facets of what I think of as the Adequan Period. The truth is, I'll always be grateful for the drug that gave us more years than we otherwise could have hoped for and a quality of life that was surprisingly good. We'd dodged another bullet and found help that appeared to have some staying power. Still, without a crystal ball, how long remained to be seen. That was unknown and subject to all of life's capricious twists and turns.

Reminders abounded that time was limited, delivered most dramatically by the now truly accelerating change in his appearance. To me it was simultaneously regal and sad. The grey was so striking now and no longer reserved for only his muzzle, spreading to the rest of his face and head. Grey was sprouting everywhere, under his flanks and inside his thighs, making a run on what had once been the inky black.

What hadn't changed, and never would, was his happiness and joy at being with us.

The smile that wowed every time I saw it.

The sweetness of that smile became a daily gift.

CHAPTER SIX
The Better Half of Old Dog Publishing

Having weathered another medical crisis we again settled into a comfortable mode. If Mac was creaky at times, well, so was I; all of us were living with the aches, pains and other charms of getting older. A new element to the kinship we felt with Mac.

Heeding the call I'd ignored most of my life, I'd now committed to writing (mostly) fulltime and launched into my first novel, Rush to Dawn. A time of high-highs and low-lows that was frightening, inspiring, rewarding, soul-crushing and truly relationship-testing depending on who you asked and on which day. Through it all, Mac was there, just outside my office, unwavering in his support.

It seemed fitting that before long I'd immortalize him in one of my novels.

How exactly did Mac become my writing partner?

It was nothing he said, but everything he never said.

I'm looking back at it now, nearly six years later. Perhaps one day, if I live long enough, I'll affectionately reminisce about those early years of a writing career that didn't end until I'd died and taken my final breath. The truth is I feel lucky having a calling and luckier still to have heeded it, making a computer keyboard my battlefield and professional home. Membership in this writers' fraternity is an honor and a privilege although the dues can be steep, financially, artistically and emotionally.

Still, with four novels and now a non-fiction book penned, more than 150 blog posts posted, and a broad scope of business writing for a couple of hundred clients in diverse industries around the world, pinch me; it's real. My personal fantasy has been legitimized. I'm doing what I was meant to do and love it wholeheartedly.

I know, without question, how lucky I am for it.

In the aggregate, my entrepreneurial and corporate adventures represented a hell of lot of years and until this point had constituted most of my working life. Following those years, the more recent ones as a marketing consultant enabled me to keep a foot and a hand in the business world, and afforded me an opportunity to dangle a toe or two in the freelancing arena.

Hanging up a writing shingle, for better or worse, let me do what I had always liked best, and what, increasingly, I came to believe I did best. I'm gratified that readers have enjoyed the novels, and the resounding appreciation of my business clients both reinforced and genuinely rewarded my efforts. But the truth is that back then as I first jumped into *Rush to Dawn*, the first Cups Drayton crime thriller, I had a bazillion questions and very few answers.

Everyone has a book in them, right? I once read in a survey that 4 out of 5 people asked that question claim to have wanted to write a book at some point in their lives.

Wanting to write a book is one thing, but discovering how to do it is quite another.

Doing it without a *Writing for Dummies* manual leaves you hoping the Force is with you.

Hardest of all is the real killer – actually doing it, pulling it off, and finishing without dropping and giving up.

Holed up in what I believe is at least a finalist for the *world's smallest office*, Mac was, as always, my constant companion. He was either snoozing outside my door, close enough for me to hear him and feel the steady rhythmic vibrations from his snoring, or hanging out in the family room I passed through any time when leaving my office.

This was his way of staying abreast of my activities.

This was a priority for Mac because being with me was his most favorite thing, and, conversely, having him around and being together was my favorite thing. However quietly I might be passing through the family room, he'd catch my vibe, raise his head, and open an eye to see what I was up to. I'd swear he'd open one eye like a NORAD-like early warning radar system that sensed me in motion.

Once that eye opened, his style was *I'm awake and coming, too* and not *I'm-sleeping-through-it-wake-me-for-dinner*. Mac was totally connected to people unlike any dog I'd had before and this was one of the ways it was so evident.

I've talked about his habit of making eye contact. He not only never looked down or away, but was totally willing to look you in the eye and, if close enough, reward you with a sloppy kiss while doing so. A number of breeders have told me that male dogs are more affectionate than females and, while I don't know if that's a fact, Mac was the most affectionate dog I've ever known. Pardon me if this sounds like some sort of doggie love fest, but I guess there's no way around the fact that's truly what it was.

Back to books.

Every book starts with a blank page one, like a newly minted Word doc.

Every writer does it differently. Some have a solid outline and know where they're going.

I don't, I have characters in their early embryonic states, with a vague idea of a story.

Counting on the characters – as I discover them – revealing the story to me.

It's worked for me. I read it was Elmore Leonard's way and that was reassuring.

The truth about writing is how much there is to learn and how intense the learning is.

Starting with coming face to face with what writing fiction was all about, what being a writer was all it about. What it meant to write every day. Figuring out how much I could do, and when to do it. When it was time to stop because it wasn't happening. When to edit, and the biggest of all: What it really means to edit. Wondering if the day would ever come when I'd fail to ask myself the question I posed every day:

Does this suck?

It isn't easy taking that hard look in the writer's mirror and facing the truth by coming to terms with strengths, and in far greater numbers, weaknesses and, worse still, an honest and open confrontation of self-indulgent tendencies. I was forced to reacquaint myself with grammar, of all things, because what I'd been too busy to pay attention to in elementary school was

MAC ALWAYS LETS THE LITTLE ONES HAVE THEIR WAY.

no longer optional. A dear friend and my pro bono editor, introduced me to wonders of the comma rather late in life, and for that I am eternally and humbly in his debt. He knows and kindly accepts that I'm still learning.

Whatever my private internal moments of doubt, those times when I questioned both my talent and my sanity for taking the plunge, Mac's affection was steadfast. He had no such doubts. Always happy to see me and never failing to boost my self-confidence with a look expressing how wonderful I was in every way. Like a cross between young children that allow fathers their heroic flashes, and a wise old friend, Mac offered his silent assurance that it was all good there was no reason to doubt my right to write. Go figure.

Mac also had an unerring sense for my mood swings and artistic ups and downs.

Laying low and allowing me space when I was rattled, but seeking me out when I was down, knowing it was better to be there for me. Calming and reassuring, there's great therapy in the act of scratching a dog's head or working his ears. However bleak things might seem, the elixir of doggie kisses and adoration are tough to argue with. Mac made me laugh, often at myself, every day of his life and more often than not took matters into his own paws.

If I was seated on the couch taking a break, he'd rush to me at full-speed, slowed only by the furniture, and thrust his head towards me, smiling and licking, with small whines and moans and a message letting me know that getting as close as possible and making it better for me was his sole priority. Thrusting his head towards me knowing that my hand would settle down over the crown of his head that fit so perfectly under it. Before long I'd work my way down to his ears, scratching behind them until he'd close his eyes and groan contentedly, then move down to his neck and throat, so big I couldn't fit both hands around, bury my face in his lush coat and then finish on to his chest and belly for the scratches he'd earned and deserved. Before I knew it, I'd be laughing and feeling better, my creative angst put aside. I'd grab his head between my two hands and thank him, get my you're welcome lick, and return to the task.

Selfless acts of kindness and from a dog no less. Truly a beautiful thing.

As I struggled to find my way as a writer and immersed myself in the process once I did, Mac had a great seat. Discovery and execution was followed by manic revisions and editing. At one point about a third of the way into the first novel, I reordered, rewrote and nearly restarted it. Like many things, you can't know at the beginning what you'll know once you've lived it and experienced it. The best reward was the agony and the ecstasy rolled-up into a final product that I truly felt great about. There were three amazing phases.

Believing you can is what gets you started.

Needing to do it is what keeps you going.

Shock and Awe rewards you when it's done.

I have felt all of that now, as well as a sense of earning membership in a rather exclusive club. As a lifelong fiction junkie, an insatiable reader and reverent fan and student of literature – pulp to timeless to transformative – the allure of actually writing had long haunted me. As if something inside mandated it and refused to be ignored, dismissed or trivialized. Confidently terrified at the prospect of doing what I'd never done, without an owner's manual, and secretly wondering if I'd actually finish the damn thing. I couldn't sleep the night after finishing the first novel. I was too excited, too … genuinely amazed that I actually had done it. But I also felt a little lost. After being consumed by the book for so long, it was suddenly over? Impossible. Unacceptable. Unnatural.

I got out of bed and went into the family room.

Mac met me, and in the middle of the night we went out for a walk.

We'd had many conversations on nearly fourteen years of walks, and I remember that one. That dark night was only nominally brightened by a nearly full moon fighting through the clouds. Few houses had lights on, and at that hour the birds were quiet. Not a single car disturbed us. Beneath the excitement was a scary and fearful reality of my reward for setting out to do what I had and then doing it: setting myself up for failure and rejection. At last, the public answers every writer's daily question:

Does this suck?

"I don't think it sucks, Mackie," I told him.

He didn't answer and I took that for his agreement.

"I can definitely do better and now I know that I can and have learned how to do it. I've already got an idea for the next book; the story continues, it will be Part Two of the trilogy."

Mac looked up, looked away, lifted his leg yet again, and *yawned*.

Perspective.

I was beyond excited. Like so many things bearing such profound personal significance, the full measure of them is revealed over time, with emotions playing starring roles. I loved the fact that as I was pouring my heart out to my dog on a middle of the night stroll around the block, and he yawned.

Back at home I went into my office.

Nowhere did I feel more at home than in this tiny computer nook just inside the mudroom entry, added-on at a time when I had no need for a home office. Lynne and I have since agreed on it as a classic moment of short-sightedness, but it turned into my place. Plus, I also loved the fact that Mac could be in his place and my place because they were appropriately juxtaposed and inextricably interconnected.

Settling into my chair, it was not yet three a.m. Mac gave me a look suggesting he wouldn't mind an early breakfast. I ignored that; he'd already pushed dinner to an earlier than imaginable time now at a mid-bordering-on-early-afternoon hour that was a little ridiculous to any that didn't know us. Breakfast now would only exaggerate the dinner problem later that day and make it worse. I told him to go back to sleep, and he yawned. Accepting the verdict, I think maybe he understood it was too early, and retired to one of his favorite spots.

When you sleep twenty hours a day it's always nap time.

I wouldn't have thought it possible, but the bond between us, the health battles we'd waged together and always would, and the friendship and joy we experienced in each other's company, had somehow grown even deeper with the years. This was startling but true.

Occasionally I had to make a short trip and was away for a few days. As was his custom when I was out of town, Lynne reported that he moped about, looked for me, and while not unhappy was clearly subdued and seemed restless and dissatisfied. I understood; when I was away I talked about him a lot.

And when I called home I wasted no time asking about him. We were best friends; completely accepting of each other, warts and all, devoted to each other in every way. We asked nothing other than to hang together and felt a certain lack of balance when we were apart.

I felt a quick pang in my heart.

How much time did we have left?

Mac was now on his way to nine years old; he was not an old dog, but was a senior dog. In people years he was 65, and had only recently overtaken me. While we were both seriously greying he looked better than ever, maintaining an utterly handsome devil quality. I loved that he was aging better than I was.

He still was the best looking male in our family.

But Mac's life had always been fragile.

Without the surgeries he would have been put down by age two or three.

For all the physical limitations, we'd had five pretty good years after the surgeries, and his remarkable personality and the dynamic nature of his interaction with us more than made up for the Labrador retriever that couldn't swim, didn't run and declined to retrieve. But if all the time to date constituted borrowed time, there was no doubt whatsoever that the hourglass of his life was running low.

I came to two rather important decisions as the first rays of daylight appeared.

First, I made it my mission and commitment to enjoy the time we had left together as completely as I could. Which meant that I'd savor each day and deny him nothing. Not that I ever had, of course, but whatever the future brought, whatever the inconveniences or medical hoops, I'd continue do whatever it took. I wanted Mac and our family to enjoy the time he had left as fully as was possible. I resolved to do everything in my power to extend that time as long as it was marked by a good quality of life and happiness in living it.

He still had a real sparkle in his eyes, and a love of life that was inarguable.

As long as that continued, we'd carry him in and out if need be.

Second, I looked at Mac and resolved to share our remarkable friendship with people neither of us would ever know. As I began the second *Cups Drayton* novel, it became clear to me Mac had a role to play. He inspired the character of 'Weller', an old, orphaned black lab.

The writing of *The Old Dog's New Trick* began as each of my novels has. I started with the characters, and with only a vague and bare-bones sense of the details of the story. Once again the characters, as I came to know and love them, revealed their story to me. I don't know if this is right, makes sense, or if it matters. I only know that it's my way and seems to work for me and it feels right.

Creating the black lab named Weller was a labor of love.

Weller is an old black lab, a little the worse for wear, malnourished, his fur matted and encrusted with mud. The old dog has been through very tough times and the miles show. On vacation camping with his people in the Mt. Hood National Forest, his owners die in a freak camp stove explosion and fire. On his own, thousands of miles from home, he has no option but to embark upon an extraordinary journey across the Cascades. He somehow makes it into the hills of Southwest Portland.

I should mention the origin of the old lab's name.

Weller is named for what is Cups', and my, favorite bourbon whisky.

A not so well known but hugely deserving 90 proof from a small but storied distillery in Kentucky, called *Weller's Special Reserve*, it's Cups' drink of choice, first appearing in *Rush to Dawn* and in my estimation is the finest comparatively cheap bourbon around.

Cups Drayton meets Weller on an early morning walk. How else?

The old dog is desperate for human contact but wary of it, mistrustful after his long journey. Cups can only get so close and the old lab is in a quandary. But as the novel starts, and Cups is settling into his new life with Evie McClary, the old dog adopts himself into the family.

It's Mac on the front cover of *The Old Dog's New Trick*, and I brought Weller back in Part Three of the trilogy, *Imperfect Resolution*. Weller will return in the next Cups Drayton thriller *Keep Going*, which I was just beginning when Mac passed. I stepped away from that story. Not that I couldn't write it or because it was too painful, but I was too close and grieving and had this story, Mac's story, to write.

In many ways, we're still grieving. It's nearly a year after Mac's passing and Lynne still finds it difficult to talk about him; more than not it brings her to tears. So you know, I'm tearing up now.

But I like talking about him, somehow it brings me closer.

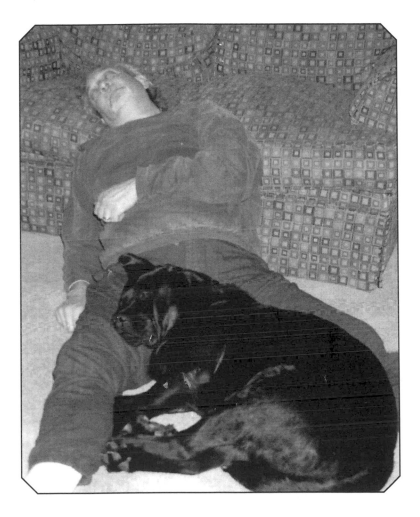

TWO OLD DOGS HARD AT WORK.

I like the fact that I've immortalized my faithful friend in the novels.

And I look forward to writing the next one and being with him again.

CHAPTER SEVEN
Mature to Senior to Elderly.

I suppose I'll never understand the tricks we allow and invite our minds to play on us. We're so eager to ignore the obvious, as if blissfully ignorant of what's to come allows us to focus on the now and indefinitely postponing the inevitable when.

Mac was no longer what I could think of as a mature dog, we'd moved past that in a relative flash, and in keeping with his role as the namesake for Old Dog Publishing, he was indeed an old dog. In keeping with the nature of the beast's too short lifespan, this also wouldn't last long.

There were three inarguable truths about these last years.

First, incredibly, he grew increasingly greyer. That handsome face showed it everywhere and his muzzle was now fully white. From his toes to his nose, white hair was appearing nearly everywhere. My favorite would always be the eyebrows that, impressively greying, lent both distinction and the false yet charming appearance, at times, of looking at you with an arched eyebrow. Suggesting that he might know something you don't

Second, while medical maintenance was an ongoing everyday affair, he was getting along better than he might have. Bursts for ill-advised short sprints out the door were fewer and from behind I could see the misalignment more clearly than ever; as if his rear end was a caboose with a mind of its own. Mac took to groaning when he got up and even more so when he lowered himself from standing to the ground. At my age I do it myself and, when I groan as a matter of course, I often think of him and smile.

And finally, in these last years and despite all that he'd been through, his smile was ever-present. His delight at seeing me was unfailingly there, and it delighted me that it was true for everyone that crossed his path: family, friends and strangers. He loved life and loved people and there was true joy in the way that he interacted with the world. Truer than ever now, I'd swear he had a sense that in many respects the life he lived was indeed a charmed one and on an intellectual inter-species platform of some kind he appreciated it. In fairness, this may have been in my head, seeing what I wanted to believe I saw, but I believed it then and believe it still.

We settled into a medical routine of Adequan shots every 28 days. Another fixture was 100mg of chewable Rimadyl twice a day. With the special, vet-only food and the dental chews I bought to help clean his teeth and freshen his breath, maintenance represented around $200 a month when he was healthy.

But as things began to happen as he aged, from time to time other maintenance items were needed. We had minor scrapes: an eye infection that required drops, and a summer where allergies hit, and I gave him an antihistamine twice a day. We had a run of few weeks where I had to treat an itchy butt he took to dragging across the rug that we never quite could attribute to anything, and ultimately it disappeared as inexplicably as it had appeared.

I learned about *hot spots* the hard way and it was scary.

Apparently, all it takes is a bite or a small puncture that gets an infection that takes off.

In Mac's case, it was a minor wound we never knew of on his upper chest, actually on his throat. I suspected he thrust his face into a bush or shrub and ran into a branch or something. An innocent, innocuous minor wound. One morning I woke, went to stroke his throat as he loved and I loved doing, and it was as if an alien life force had taken up residence. Ugly, too, with secretions making his fur thick, and oddly clumped together, the outward manifestations of an infection that also produced a high fever. I remember racing to the vet at 8 am on a Saturday morning before they opened and pounding on the back door, sensing that this surprise ailment was serious. Serious it was, and he spent a couple of nights at the vet, with the fur shaved, a cone, and medicated with antibiotics topically and internally. To avoid irritation, we also exchanged his regular chain collar for a red harness used only on walks with a leash.

It was always something, but one summer when he was ten there was a bigger scare.

Early one morning I got up as usual, fed Mac as usual, he scarfed it down as usual, we took our walk as usual, and came inside as usual.

When my son, Jake, appeared not long after, Mac went to the door to be let out, as usual. Minutes later Jake found me in my office.

"Dad, I'm not sure, but something might be up with Mac," he told me.

"Why do you say that?" I asked.

"I let him out and he immediately threw up his breakfast in the grass."

I went out to have a look, expecting to find the telltale signs of vomiting after eating grass. That happened from time to time but there was none of that. This was unlike Mac. He never threw up breakfast; and there was more. He'd rushed outside to the grass – usually when he did throw up in was just *inside*. And he looked like he didn't feel well which almost never happened.

"What are we going to do, Dad?" Jake asked.

"I'm going to take him to the vet. You're right; something's up and I'm glad you said something."

Our vet did an ultrasound but it was inclusive.

After discussing it with her, I took him over to Dr. H.'s referral clinic for a higher-end, and much, much more expensive ultrasound. The blockage diagnosis was confirmed and if we got lucky he'd pass it, and if not, the only other option was surgery. The plan was to keep Mac there for a day or two, watching him closely, while I sat at home with my fingers crossed waiting for it to pass and the phone to ring.

When it did, we were indeed lucky.

"He passed it," Dr. H. told me. "I was beginning to wonder, but he did. He can go home tomorrow. I want to keep him overnight to be safe, just in case there's more."

"What was it?" I asked.

"It almost looks like a piece of neutral colored fabric," he answered, "Ring a bell with you?"

It didn't at first but did later.

For years I'd given Mac old comforters as bedding in his kennel. He loved to chew them and tear the ticking out. Whenever I washed his bedding or cleaned his kennel, there were handfuls of ticking to collect, along with tiny scraps of fabric. He never ate them but worked at it with enthusiasm, and I'd come to believe it was how he settled down for the night, occupied himself if he woke up, or amused himself on the rare occasions he was closed up in his kennel during the day.

It didn't make sense.

Then I realized that something I'd done might have been at the heart of it.

Occasionally, when a repair technician came to the house to do some work on the furnace or cable, and they preferred not to have a large, overly-affectionate old lab assist them, I'd grab one of his bones, often filled with peanut butter, or a couple of biscuits, and toss them into his kennel as a treat to enjoy while we uncharacteristically locked him away.

The problem was that Mac was perpetually hungry, and the standing joke was that he'd eat anything at any time that even remotely resembled food. Now it made sense. All it would take was a little peanut butter from one of the stuffed shank bones, or a few biscuit crumbs stuck to a piece of fabric and he'd inhale it without hesitation.

From that point forward I never again allowed anything that resembled food into his kennel. I was relieved, genuinely thankful that intestinal surgery wasn't needed for the blockage, and that at his age I hadn't been forced to make the call.

But dodging that bullet had been anything but inexpensive. Between two vets, two ultrasounds, x-rays and four nights of care, the cost was around $2000.

The following spring there was another scare.

Cancer.

One very pleasant and incredibly generous byproduct of trips to the vet every four weeks was that Mac got a quick check-up. By this time he'd been granted nothing less than rock star status at the clinic. My vet had grown to genuinely love Mac and he was a staff favorite. So after his injection she'd look into his eyes, ears and run her hands over him.

On one of those occasions she found a lump on his side and it wasn't one of the fatty tumors so common to older dogs. A quick biopsy prompted lab tests that told her it was mast cell skin cancer, and, while this was surgery we couldn't avoid, it was also a procedure that he could handle. So we had it done, and a couple of days afterwards brought him home. Like people, there were drainage issues. Like a dog, he'd wear a plastic cone over his head so he couldn't get at the stiches.

I'd treat the wound with ointments topically and antibiotics internally.

My vet also advised keeping him contained in one room. That was easy – the family room was where he lived most of the time.

Also recommended were plastic sheets over the carpet. It's a large room, about 400 square feet, and that meant a lot of plastic, and general weirdness for a couple of weeks. None of that mattered, we were hardly inexperienced newbies when it came to doggie post-surgical care. When the lab tests of what they'd removed came back as benign, and a veterinary

oncologist saw no reason for further concern, it was a triumphant and happy day for all of us.

Almost enough to take the sting out of our latest vet bill.

I remember once, thinking about all of Mac's medical expenses, and tallied them up, loosely in my head. That aggregate tab, what I'd always thought of as on a par with freshman and sophomore years at the University of Oregon, just kept growing. For all of it, only one thought came to mind.

Mac had been worth every penny.

And the profound lifestyle adjustments large and small, no big deal. I sensed there were more to come now, because Mac had indeed transitioned from mature to senior and was now what I thought of as elderly. It became impossible for me not to think of it, and I was shocked at how much we'd experienced, amazed at how quickly the years had flown by.

There were certain things we or he simply didn't do anymore. For years he'd seize the opportunity for a nap on the loveseat in the family room. He knew better but he also knew we'd make a fuss and make him get down, but nothing beyond that. But he was also now stone deaf. He no longer heard us coming and was caught in the act trying to get down in time before being busted. Now Mac slept through it and was startled by us waking him from a nap curled up on the loveseat.

We often let him sleep on without disturbing him.

Then one day he could no longer haul himself up on the loveseat.

There would be a series of things he used to do but didn't any more.

Starting with walking him to that coffee shop not far

from our house on Sundays. All the years sitting outside in all kinds of weather, Mac at our feet, a fixture on so many Sunday mornings. At first, when the walks became too much, I'd load him in the car and subject him to short a car trip because he so genuinely loved being there and seeing people.

Until even that became too much. We miss those days.

Years of family excursions in the fall to the Hood River Valley for apples, one of the few car trips with him we stubbornly tried to avoid discontinuing, finally ended and Mac now stayed at home. Now it was only Lynne and me; no kids and no dog. A sign of the new order of things as we made the annual trek each October to our favorite orchard for recently harvested apples. Fuji apples from Hood River are my personal favorite and for the rest of my life will remind me of Mac.

All those years with our kids and Mac loaded in the car, heading east out of Portland to Sandy, Oregon with a stop at Joe's Donuts, over sixty years of the best glazed and jelly donuts I've ever had. Up US 26 around Mt. Hood, and just past the summit, OR 35 to Parkdale, home to our favorite orchard. Loading the trunk with more apples than we realized and more than we'd ever eat. Continuing down through the Hood River Valley into Hood River, the wind surfing capitol of the world on the banks of the Columbia River in the heart of the Columbia River Gorge, before driving home. On the way we'd stop at Cascade Locks, to have lunch at Char-Burger, and let Mac and the boys play in the remarkable city park.

Happy times then, but Mac had now more than ever reached a point where he'd acquiesced despite never being a fan of the car, now more than ever. So there would no longer be a trip where refusing to lie down he'd stand the entire way and return home stiff, exhausted and limping. This was a sentimental jolt and another signal. We hated not having him with us, but hated the price he paid for it and would no longer ask him to.

When we'd go on vacation, Mac spent time – always happily – at local kennels. His health was such that I became increasingly uncomfortable with trusting a kennel, and my vet once again came to the rescue. Their clinic only boarded dogs and cats that were staying overnight for medical reasons, they weren't a boarding clinic.

For Mac they made an exception.

They were always willing to board him and he was always delighted by a chance to visit.

It was wonderful knowing they'd shower him with attention and affection.

And in the event of a medical crisis, he was right where he needed to be.

So I slept better and worried less when we were away.

Emphasis on *worried less* but I still worried.

The reality was that in many ways both large and small, the inevitable mortality of our four-legged pal was rearing its ugly head more emphatically every day now. A pet's short, and bittersweet life expectancies seem a reasonable price to pay … until time comes to pay it.

At thirteen he waddled more than walked, taking his own sweet time in the process. His favorite spot next to Lynne on the deck as she read in nice weather was no longer accessible from the yard; he'd reached a point where he couldn't jump up from the side, but needed assistance. Every day we were reminded of the heartbreaking end of life drawing nearer.

Large breeds typically live shorter lives, and a dog with a medical past like Mac's was certainly a prime candidate for a shorter one. It had been nearly thirteen years since medical issues had threatened Mac's life. Miraculously, or thanks to so many of us that loved him so deeply, the old guy had survived to live a doggone good old dog's life.

Incredibly, now over thirteen years, he'd beaten the odds and exceeded all reasonable expectations. I began to think of this as bonus time. He was very old, he was very creaky, but he wasn't fragile and for the moment, not sickly.

In a way, we'd been lucky, and I remember saying that at dinner one night.

Lynne looked at me like I was crazy.

"What you, what we've all done, is the reason behind it, not luck," she commented.

And I couldn't deny the truth of it.

We had made our luck, but now the enemy was old age and from that bullet there was no dodging, no hiding and no escape. Now part of each day, consciously or not, was preparing for what we simply can't prepare for. His eyes still sparkled and shone with love but his face had a look of old age and the limitations of his body could no longer be ignored,

There were still more adjustments to come.

CHAPTER EIGHT
Mac's Final Months

This is the dog I'd taken to describing as the dog of my life and the finest dog I'll ever know and the truth is I meant and wholeheartedly believed every word of it. But now Mac was thirteen going on fourteen and at that age there are no remaining illusions about where you are. The simple fact is that the end is near.

There is no longer *if*. There is only *when*.

Indulge me in an oh-so-brief philosophical moment.

This is no attempt to define or persuade, but an effort to provide context for the whirlwind of thoughts, feelings and emotions that consumed me at the time.

Death and the end of life is a helluva subject, with no shortage of literature and opinion, spiritual and secular. From early man's first self-conscious thoughts, human beings have freely espoused on the topic, in an infinite variety of ways by infinitely diverse people and I suppose for infinitely different reasons; from comfort to closure. Viewed as simply the end or as a joyous and hopeful beginning, or perhaps fulfilling a basic human need to understand what we don't or can't.

The debate, perhaps the very oldest debate of all, rages on and maybe it always will.

It occurred to me that what we can learn from our experiences with death, saying our last goodbyes to those we love, may ultimately be of practical day to day value for those left behind. In confronting the end of Mac's life, I wanted to spare myself pain, if possible, and prepare as best I could, if possible. I saw the death experience for survivors in three distinct stages; before, during and after. For the wide differences of opinion, it seemed what can't be argued is that our fear and dread of the end, particularly if we're watching it draw nearer from a front-row seat, flavors what time remains and how hard that is to prevent. With so much out of my control, it seemed reasonable to take a stab at doing something about that.

Rationally, it seemed absurd to think I'd be immune and get a pass, but I would give it my best effort. My attempt began with a well-intended determination to enjoy to the fullest the time we had left. I had neither the desire to suffer in advance nor to kid myself that there was much time left. I vowed not to indulge in morbid thoughts that by definition steal from the sweetness of the present. I'd lived long enough to witness and experience how brave fronts like that have a way of crumbling easily when we least expect it.

The intellectual me resolved to not allow it and make the most of every day.

The emotional me doubted there was anything I could do to stop it.

We weren't on death watch; in fact, it was more the opposite as Halloween 2013 neared, enjoying a bit of a respite from medical crises. Mac, while not frail, had certainly become elderly in both his actions and appearance. I knew better than to take it for granted, knowing that like a lull in a storm it can change to fury in an instant. For the moment, although slower and creakier, he was his affectionate self and I made it a point to enjoy him; taking his head in my hands and thrusting my face in his for the kisses that he loved so much and never failed to deliver.

I encouraged him to roll to his back for belly scratches, and plopping myself down on the floor in front of the couch in the family room with my legs spread so he could curl up between them as he'd done all his life – a routine I'd come to see as what passed for a big ole lab's way of being a lap dog. The position is shown in the picture of the two of us asleep that I call *Old Dogs at Work*. For all of his life, wherever he was, when I hit the floor like that he made his way over for what had given us moments of intimate closeness and affection precious to us both.

The moments still came but only very occasionally; no disguising things were changing.

One of the differences is that I was looking for signs.

Late in the afternoon on Halloween I got one.

Coming out of my office I have a clear view to the back yard. Mac was nowhere to be found inside and when I looked out that way and I saw him right away.

Seated, more prone on the ground, struggling to get up but unable to.

Slipping into my well-worn dog-walking boat shoes, I went out to him.

He looked up, and his expression wasn't so much distress

but surprise, perhaps even a little chagrined, that what he was trying to do he couldn't do no matter how hard he tried. He looked older than ever, and all I wanted was to get him up, hope that he stayed up, and even more wishing for this to be an anomaly, merely an isolated event and not a first glimpse at the newest normal.

"Mackie, my baby boy," I said bending down to him, "looks like you're having a time. Let's help you up, buddy."

As I reached under him to lift his back legs, he gave me his famous ear-lick, and I had to laugh. He never missed a chance. Sloppy, messy and wet, I'd give anything for just one more.

Mac stood and followed me as I turned to return from the yard to the family room.

He walked slowly but without incident, at a speed I'd describe as somewhere between glacial and molasses, a speed that had become his custom.

"You really are a lumbering old lab these days," I said, opening the door for him, "Still a handsome devil, too, old boy."

It was late afternoon on Halloween day, and Lynne and I – *Nonni and Babbo*, had planned to run over to our oldest son's house to see grandkids in costume before they went out trick or treating, in time for me to get home in time to man the door as I'd done for so many years. Nonni went without me.

I'd stay at home, closer to Mac, just in case.

Lynne saw the worry I couldn't hide and may have thought I was overreacting again. If she did, these were thoughts she kept to herself. It was a question I was indeed asking myself. In my mind, perhaps because as Mac's primary caregiver I was so involved and attuned to his every activity every day, I knew I wasn't overreacting this time. The Grim Doggie Reaper wasn't stalking us that day, but I had no doubt that he'd added us to his manifest.

I didn't know it then, but surely suspected, that this would be the beginning of the last new Mac normal for me. Things I wouldn't do, places I wouldn't go, vacations the family would take without me, balking at joining them because I was no longer comfortable leaving him as I once had, even with our vet. As a boy, our family was away on vacation when my first dog, Bonnie, died. When we came home my dad was devastated. I'm not sure he ever got over it and blamed himself in a way I understood. I wanted none of that.

Over the next couple of months, the getting-up episode in the back yard was repeated a few times. While not an everyday occurrence, it was a regularly irregular interruption that came without notice. For all of that, Mac's basic lifestyle was barely impacted. He did what he always did; eating, sleeping, following us around to be wherever we were, along with whatever trips to the vet medical tending that was required at the moment.

But while Mac, on a base level, was doing okay, the decline was evident in less obvious ways. Evan often came over with his delightful Cocker mix; a one-eyed sweetheart named Tulip. Tulip was more excited to see Mac than vice versa, and more and more he was mostly disinterested. Tulee developed a fixation for his cherished bones, and if she nabbed one, he let it go. Small and insignificant changes in behavior that really weren't so insignificant after all. They confirmed what was new in a future I didn't want to face but had no choice in the matter.

Just before Thanksgiving, we learned that Lynne's uncle in Los Angeles was planning to bring the entire family in for a year-end family reunion at a resort in Southern California. Flying out Christmas morning, four days and three nights, it was made clear to me that this was a special event where my attendance was not optional.

A family reunion and I had to go.

More than a little upsetting for a couple of different reasons.

In all my life I'd never been away from home during the Holidays. The thought of that, alone, made me a bit uneasy. An all-expenses paid trip to La La Land couldn't be denied, Lynne's uncle was providing an once-in-a-lifetime trip, but it seemed unnatural. Not only would we be away from home, but we'd be in warm weather with palm trees where Christmas lights simply didn't compute.

And then there was Mac.

I hated the thought of being away, but more than just me, that everyone that would be away. But my vet agreed without hesitation to watch Mac.

"You'll have to bring him Christmas Eve and we close early," she said kindly. "That's an extra night. And we're closed Christmas Day, but we'll have a doc on call and techs here for the basics."

"Truly appreciate that. Makes me nervous but I have no choice," I confessed, "I have to go."

"And you should go. Don't worry. I'll be on call," she added. "Mac'll be fine."

"I hope so. I know so. It's just … he's so old. Worrying is in my DNA."

Worry I did, and called a few times to get updates.

Back in Portland, when I picked him up and brought him home, the entire family rejoiced in a family reunion after the family reunion. It was one we all celebrated joyfully and with total relief.

I wasn't the only one who had worried while we were away. All of us had.

New Year's Eve came along with our annual open house to celebrate the holiday and Lynne's birthday. Large groups, crowded rooms and hallways, food everywhere and it made sense not have Mac underfoot to boot, so for all those years we'd banished Mac from attending.

We'd always set him up rather nicely.

A snug and warm place where he had a *legal loveseat* in the shed, aka rehearsal space for Jake's band, *The Shedmen*. Unknown to us, years ago our son Evan had allowed Mac free rein to the loveseat in the shed during high school. No wonder Mac never took our ban on the family room loveseat to heart. In any event, with food, water and a bone, he was happy enough in the shed. For me the highpoint of the night was bringing him back inside after the party.

This year I insisted on a different approach.

No shed. He'd be with us.

No discussion.

If our guests didn't like it, too bad.

They could leave, but Mackie stayed.

Lynne agreed and I swear the party that year was cheerier for his presence.

Not long after the Holidays, in early January something happened that fundamentally changed everything. A staple of daily life every day of Mac's life – and mine – became a memory that haunts me still, albeit in a bittersweet and almost endearing way.

I didn't know it at the time, but that day we took our very last walk together.

Mac still lived for walks as he always had, and we took one every morning as we always had.

Sick or well, too busy, in the mood or not, every day. In torrential, pouring rain, and in Oregon there's plenty of it; on days when it's a dry heat didn't matter; during fierce snowstorms; after one of the Northwest's famed *Silver Thaws* sliding precariously over sheets of ice covering everything everywhere. Those were particularly unnerving because Mac's bionic joints in all his legs hadn't made him *better* like Steve Austin in the Six Million Dollar Man. But he expected his walk, he needed his walk and he'd get it.

I saved the file I was working on and, leaving my office, walked to the kitchen to grab a light lunch. Mac was in one of his favorite spots; sleeping on the threshold between the family room and the kitchen. As I walked by, he got up and followed me into the kitchen, sneaking by before I remembered to close the door, amenable to shifting to one of his favorite spots on the floors warmed by radiant heat that he loved so much.

My eyes followed him in and something unusual grabbed my attention.

It was red. A serious spot of blood on the carpet in the threshold.

Bright, vivid and startling. Fresh and I remember vital coming to mind but don't know why. It just struck me that way.

A quick look, as if I knew what to look for, told me nothing more. I couldn't find the source and this time what I felt would definitely be described as all-out real panic. Fear, actually. I got his harness and leash and prepared to load him in the car. I called our vet and let them know we were on our way. The blood scared the hell out of me. I wondered if this was it.

This was not it.

It turned out that he'd snagged a nail on his rear right paw, and split it totally. They had to remove the nail, and bandage the entire paw; it would be bandaged for a couple of weeks. During that time he'd wear doggie booties outside, to keep it clean and dry.

"No walks," my vet told me.

"He loves them so much, has demanded them every day of his life. Remember Weller, the old lab in my crime thrillers?" I asked the vet. "Cups walks Weller and you know that's Mac and me. Still, I can't dismiss that maybe it's time; so often he's limping, barely making it home, and his joints seizing-up. Maybe not taking them now is the way to wean him from walks. God, I hate the thought of it."

"It might be time," our vet said softly.

Another sign, I thought.

"You know Mac will be fourteen in July – if he makes it," I said. "The incredible thing, and it's always been what's so … amazing, no, remarkable, is he's still so happy with his life. He accepts, never holds a grudge and still makes me laugh every day."

"I'm betting he'll make it," she said.

I sighed. "My last two dogs did, I'd like Mac to, especially because once upon a time, about thirteen years ago, I didn't know if he'd make it to two. What a life, what a happy life. What a pure spirit he is, happy just to love us – and everyone he meets. I admire that. I envy that."

Then my vet said something that touched me deeply, adding context that perhaps I'd never consciously considered before.

"He is a pure spirit and what a beautiful world it would be if we all could live like that."

"If we could love like that," I added, jumping in. "And accept. And forgive."

So our walks after nearly fourteen years became history.

More and more we'd help him when the floors were too slippery for him to gain traction, or his legs too weak to support his still massive bulk.

When Lynne went out to the deck to read, if Mac wanted to join her, we escorted him through the house. The days of his going around and climbing onto to the deck were another piece of history, and coming through the house the best and only way to get him there now. And these days he didn't stay long; his appearances on the deck with Lynne more cameo-like. We joked about how long it took to take him such a short distance back and forth.

More than once a struggling moment with Mac scared the hell out of me.

I got better at dealing with them but never got used to them.

We weren't living an emergency, but increasingly I had the feeling of always being on the verge of one. That at any time, this might be it. Every morning I awoke wondering if he'd passed a pleasant night or had passed during the night.

The drugs for his joints didn't appear to be helping at all now.

I'm not sure if the Cartrophen, the latest veterinary advance to treat arthritis in dogs that I'd added to Adequan for the last year, ever did help. Vets bought it in Canada and results had been very good. We'd tried it but found it too late but I'm happy that it's helping other dogs.

I'd even tried adding Black Strap Molasses to his food after reading about it on a dog forum.

With Mac's fourteenth birthday only two calendar turns away, Jake, our youngest son, spoke hopefully that he had a couple of years left in him. I would have wished to believe that was possible, but knew that at this point there was absolutely no way. The decline was so clear to me, as was the fact that all the drugs were now apparently for naught.

Nothing appeared to help, and although he was slowing down, and wasn't yet breaking down or shutting down as vets call it, making it to fourteen, it seemed to me, would be no small feat.

My two previous dogs, Dapper and Ozzie, had made it to fourteen.

I was hoping Mac would make it, too.

Part of me doubted he could.

But part of me knew better than to bet against him.

CHAPTER NINE
The Old Dog's Last Days and Final Gifts

Mac's 14th birthday was only a little over a month away, but his decline was more evident daily in the help he routinely needed more and more, getting up both inside and outside. So, Crying Wolf aside, I had no doubt the end was close, and cried more than once facing the truth of it. I can't decide which is worse: The pain of saying goodbye to someone we love or the anticipation that we soon will be. Some choice.

A month earlier I hadn't thought it possible for him to move any more slowly, but he was. On his rare trips from one end of the house to the other, even the distinctive clicking of his nails on the floors that had always delighted us had a distinctively slower pacing. We'd hear him coming and could only smile as it seemed to take forever for the old guy to arrive.

A fine late day in May. In Oregon, the rainy season hadn't ended completely, but we never know when or if it would. There's the rub in this beautiful part of the world. Winters are wet, but it rolls off; we don't have to scrape it off. Summers are glorious, and in good years we enjoy long stretches of what I've always thought of as *Chamber of Commerce Weather*. Summer, if shorter and slow to arrive some years, is well worth the wait. Coming from the Midwest I was an eager and willing convert to the land of heat without humidity.

Oregon has four seasons on a flexible and unknown schedule. Like seasonal shape-shifters under the umbrella of two great Super Seasons: Rainy and Dry. The wet you accept and endure because the dry is glorious. The annual question is when will it stop raining and when will summer come and opinions fall into three buckets. *Optimists* say June, but I've been here long enough to know June is no certainty. *Realists* insist that July 5th is clearly the official unofficial start to our summer, *after* a soggy Fourth. The *Cynics* amongst us joke that Labor Day may be the safer bet, and we Oregonians collectively wince but don't protest with much conviction, as Fatalists recall years when summer went MIA and never arrived. I've seen one or two.

They're tough.

This day, however, was a dandy. Low sixties with a few sunbreaks in the clouds and no showers is a fine day in May. I opened the windows and the sliding screen doggie door that offered Mac in-and-out freedom to the yard if he was of a mind. All his life he'd loved to sit on the patio just outside the screen, where he could be outside with a clear view inside to ensure he didn't miss anything.

For the first time ever he didn't seem to have much interest.

Another sign. So many lately. I feared I could only steel my heart so many times before, without warning, one of these moments would simply be too much. In recent weeks there had been a couple of them that prompted calls to the vet, asking if there was anything else we could possibly do but knowing there really wasn't anything left to do. I'd been down that road and it appeared we'd exhausted everything. I no longer took good-natured ribbing from the family about over-reacting; we all tried not to.

But that pleasant afternoon, Mac had real trouble getting up and my attempts to assist weren't enough to keep him up. I'd recently purchased a sling, the latest and what would be the last in the line of doggie accessories you'd never think of needing. I bought it for the help I needed getting him in and out of the car to go to the vet for his shots. Now I didn't think there would be any more shots, those drugs no longer seemed to matter, but I sure needed the sling now to get him up and back inside. His legs just didn't have enough strength. I briefly left him in the yard and went to get it along with his harness and leash.

"I'll be right back, buddy," I said, and he lowered his head to the ground.

Returning, I said, "Let's get you up and into the house, Mackie," and slipped the sling under and around his midsection.

I lifted him up, and held him up, keeping most of his weight off his back legs as I guided him the short distance to the house. Inside, he seemed to be moving slightly better, able to stand, although I doubted for long, and it was late enough for his dinner. All his life food had been the ultimate incentive and now it was all I had to offer.

I called the vet as he ate. Even after four dogs, the big question was so hard to answer.

How do you really know when?

My vet was on vacation, and her partner was taking her calls. Everyone at the clinic knew us, and after emotionally identifying myself and explained why I calling, was put right through to him. We got priority treatment and I was truly grateful for it.

"What's up?" he asked. "Mac not doing well?"

He listened silently as I told him, and when I finished I asked the How Do I know question. Interestingly, his take was somewhat different from his partner. Different opinions and I understood both points of view, but he said something I hadn't heard before. Something that, for the first time in a long time, gave me just the faintest glimmer of hope.

A chance, however slim, was more than welcome and I'd pounce on it.

"Here's what I think, and I'll say right off that not everyone agrees with me," he began. "Dr. E. and I don't on this. As far as Mac today, I'm guessing he's much weaker than when she saw him last, and she might feel differently if she were here. I saw him in passing a couple of weeks ago, but from what I'm hearing from you, things have gone downhill since then."

"That's right, they have and I'm all ears," I said. "Tell me."

"Steroids. Prednisone. Here's my take on it with a little background. You ask me when? A veterinary professor told me back in Vet School that he thought no old dog should be put down without giving steroids a try. I've seen happy results many times. Less pain, they're more comfortable and sometimes far more mobile. Some get a second chance, even a couple of years. Side effects, yeah, sometimes; that's Dr. E's objection. But …"

"He's not playing major league baseball, and he's at the end of his career," I interrupted him. "Side effects mean little to me. We're at the end, clearly. It's a shot, our only shot. I didn't think I had any shot and I want them. Now."

"Mac's a little over 100 pounds, still? He asked.

"In that neighborhood."

"I'll fill it now, and give you a week's worth. Dr. E. will be back before then, and you can discuss with her whether to continue. We'll have it ready before you get here."

Excited by the prospect, I drove immediately to the clinic, picked up the medicine and returned home. I was looking for a miracle, even a tiny one, and couldn't wait to construct one of my famous *peanut butter breadie-ball pill delivery vehicles* and see what happened. Something was better than nothing and I was truly grateful that at the eleventh hour we had a something.

And it worked.

Mac perked up. He moved around better, seemed to be in less pain, and had more mobility and maybe even a bit more energy. He began going in and out, using the sliding screen door again when it was available, and without the episodes getting stuck outside unable to get up. Those were happier days, a little shelter and calm before the storm that has been steadily brewing for some time now. As a family we were all delighted by those days, hoping they'd go on for a good long time. That Mac would be one of those lucky dogs that got a bonus year or two.

He wasn't one of those lucky ones.

We got a couple of bittersweet weeks and then the prednisone no longer helped.

The signs of the inevitable had returned and with rather

dramatic emphasis after what had proved to be a brief respite, a short-lived improvement. Back to barely making it around and in need of help in and out and up and down just about always.

"Here's the big question," I said to Lynne one morning in early June.

"What?"

"Dr. E. will come to house when it's time. I'm not taking him in, no need for it and he doesn't need the stress. But how do I know when to call?"

"He'll tell us," she said without hesitation.

"You think?" I asked.

"I do. Mackie will give us a sign," she said, and put her hands to her mouth and cried.

"You're right, he will," I agreed, and joined her, hugged her, as we cried together.

Poor deaf Mac, always sensitive to my emotional state, couldn't hear us, of course, but must have caught the vibe because he'd lifted his head, and was eyeing us with concern on his face. Those most beautiful deep brown eyes, almost dark chocolate, looked a bit duller to me.

I handed Lynne a Kleenex, took one for myself, and we gathered ourselves. Taking deep breaths, blowing our noses, laughing at ourselves. We'd raised four children, had five grandchildren, lost parents, friends and seen enough of life's ups and downs to avoid going to pieces over an old black Lab. We could avoid that, couldn't we?

Of course we couldn't.

Lynne went to Mac, lying on the rug by his bowls in front of his kennel. Since that gut-wrenching struggle to get him inside, he hadn't really moved. I knew beyond any doubt whatsoever, he was shutting down.

The question that for so long I couldn't answer would be answered soon.

I bent down to him and then sat down by him and wrapped my arms around his head.

He gave me the slightest lick on the ear and I buried my face in his warm fur. The blackest of black as a puppy, flecked with grey just about everywhere now. Still handsome, but so old.

"Mackie, my best baby boy," I began, gently lifting up his head. "There's just nothing left, nothing more I can do, man. If there was we would, but there just isn't." Like a child, with no one around, I kissed him on his nose as tears ran freely down the sides of my face.

So little time left, I knew, and his birthday was only a week away. I decided to ask my vet if I could increase the steroids, because why not, as my father-in-law used to say, Couldn't hoit. Not that I held out much hope for it, but felt it might make his last days a bit more comfortable. So I did, although it made only a nominal difference. Now he needed help going in and out every time. Now everything now was extra work, but I was more than willing. We all were.

This was Mackie.

He hung on another week and made it to his fourteenth birthday.

No gifts, no cake, but Lynne prepared a ground beef and rice meal that he ate up.

Slower than usual, but he ate it.

The next morning, a day after his birthday, I'd write his

annual birthday post.

And knew it was the last birthday post.

Happy as I'd be to write it, I'd leave tears on my keyboard.

The next morning I awoke and went into the family room wondering as I did each day what I'd find. I found Mac awake and somewhat interested in breakfast. Somewhat, he was never anything less than gung-ho about breakfast until that day. He ate half, in itself a sign, but I didn't dwell on it. Signs didn't matter as much now. I'd stepped-up steroids, but if they had helped at all it was just a little. But we'd given it a try and thankfully I had no regrets or second thoughts. I liked knowing that.

He was still with us.

He'd made it to fourteen, after all.

And further proof was he stood to eat, and actually went out on his own.

A pleasant surprise that made no sense, but it was good to see.

Still, I went with him and after he took one of his usually impressive Number One's, I used the sling to keep him up and steady for a Number Two. Getting in position had become harder the last few months, as if his hips were saying enough.

Incredibly, afterwards he came back into the house on his own, although I was nearby standing-by, and lay down on the rug in front of his kennel, by his bowls. As he seemed comparatively okay, I went into my office to do some work. That had been tough for me to do in recent days.

A day after he turned fourteen, I wrote and posted Mac's 14th Birthday Post. It was titled 'The Old Dog Hobbles to Fourteen'.

I'd posted it a few days later than usual, but lately life had been altered more than usual.

Lynne was working out at the gym, and wouldn't be home for a while. She often went to coffee afterwards with her gym friends. It had been four hours or so since Mac had been out, and proactively hard-wired to his cycles and needs, I decided it was time to assist him in and out, hoping he'd more comfortable.

Which I did and now, looking back at nearly fourteen years in its entirety, the ups and downs and scary moments in so many different ways, experienced what was unquestionably the absolute worst of all. I got him up with the sling, and nudged-urged and steered him outside. When we made it to the grass, he went down, without doing anything, and couldn't get up. Then, even with my help up, he couldn't stay up. I worked him back inside, hating myself because I was struggling to get Mac back inside, dragging more than anything. He was like 105 pounds of awkward dead weight. Expediency and whatever worked was all I had and trumped all to do it. As kindly as I could, as gently as I could, and I wish I'd been capable of better, finally did get him inside. I was breathing hard, caused by the exertion and the emotion of maneuvering him back onto the rug in front of his kennel. Returning him to where I'd interrupted him minutes before, and good intentions notwithstanding wishing I hadn't ever done that.

This was, I knew, *it*.

When was *now*.

Living with that unanswered question for so long and bang: answered.

All kinds of thoughts hit me, including one that was all-encompassing.

Another sad twist on old news new again. News that broke when he was not quite a year-old, of chronic, and usually fatal, joint problems in all four legs. We'd been on watch for this moment for over thirteen years.

And now, a day after turning fourteen here it was. I knew.

For the first time in his life, Mac didn't have the sparkle that had radiated from him every moment of his life. A sparkle, the product of his love of life, that, even during surgeries and all the assorted medical adventures, never stopped coming, had transcended simply everything.

Always.

Loving and trusting life every day, the people-centric lab had lived a remarkable life despite long odds, happy and grateful for it in his way. I wonder if he had a mission on some level, preferring people, all people, and giving the non-dog lovers amongst us his very best. Giving those folks a charitable pass and a little extra something to win them over.

He loved his family so enthusiastically and unconditionally, that it was particularly touching when he reunited with our grown kids returning home after college, or living out of town, or deployments in Iraq and Afghanistan; seeing them less but never loving them less.

And for all the love he showed for all of us, there was something special he gave me.

For fourteen years and a day, I'd been the wealthiest dog lover on Earth.

I'm not meaning to imply you aren't; I hope you are. I know I was.

Lynne would be home from the gym soon. I phoned the vet.

I don't exactly remember the call, but know I talked with Dr. E., and in her kind and considerate way she immediately offered to come to the house at 7 pm. With eight hours before she arrived there were things to do.

Back home after her morning workout, Lynne came into the family room. I said nothing, but as she has done so skillfully for nearly thirty-four years, she read me perfectly.

"What?" she asked.

"This is the day," I answered, "Just as you said last week. God, it was just last week, but Mackie's telling us; he's given us the sign."

Without commenting, she went over to him, got down on her knees to be with him and looked into his eyes. After spending a minute or two, she got up and came to me, saying, "He's telling us all right," started to cry. It was a few moments before she was able to finish, "The sparkle is gone. God, it really is. What now?"

"I've already made the call. Dr. E. is coming at 7."

"The boys," Lynne said tonelessly.

I wondered if the empathy she felt for what our boys would experience over this was even greater than her concern for our own. I knew the answer, it was both. And that said so much. She is an extraordinary mother and Nonni, giving as much of herself and loving as hard as anyone I've ever known. Her love for Mac, and the richness of her relationship with a dog was something she had never expected. I was always the dog lover. Mac turned her into one.

She had become a convert of the absolute highest order,

loving that dog so passionately and completely, and, over these last years, spending more time with him, just the two of them, than anyone other than me. She'd become Mac's Mom to my Dad. We thought of him as our fifth child and fourth son in a way that seemed natural. Their afternoons on the deck their time together was Mac's favorite thing to do with her, as he'd had favorite things with other people in his life who were important.

"The boys," she said again, and I realized I'd been lost in my thoughts.

"Yeah, the boys – I'll let them know."

I sent emails and texts. I knew I couldn't keep it together on the phone.

Mackie's struggling. Come say goodbye if you can. The vet is coming at seven.

Waiting, time passing so slowly and always on the verge of tears.

Our boys had amazing relationships with Mac. They'd all make it as soon as possible.

I thought of those precious relationships. Each loved him fiercely. Evan, our soldier son, deployed in Iraq and Afghanistan for nearly three years, unfailingly asked about Mac, *first*, on his calls to us, and when he stateside again visited regularly. Jake, our youngest and recently graduated from the U of O, had lived with Mac most of his life, and since graduating spent more time with him than anyone but Lynne and me. The older kids saw him when they could and it was always great fun to watch.

Time was passing more slowly than ever, absurdly slowly. In my mind, possessing me, was the image of our vet arriving at the front door. I couldn't force it away, couldn't do anything else but return to it, caught in an endlessly cycling loop, feeling trapped in a time warp and at total loose ends.

Nothing made sense; how could it?

Mac was neither responsive nor unresponsive, just disengaged and uninterested; a first for Mac.

Ah, so many firsts, and I wondered how many more firsts lay ahead.

Evan rescued us in mid-afternoon, arriving with his loving strength that buttressed and comforted Lynne and me. As a decorated combat engineer in two wars, decommissioning tons of enemy explosives in hundreds of buildings across two war zones as the 82nd supported Special Ops, he was no stranger to the end of life. And although I don't know if anyone could have loved this dog more deeply than he did, I admired – even envied – that his experience seemed to make him less fragile than me.

Anyone would have been less fragile than how I felt inside. I've got a cream filling; I'm a sentimental softie. Proud of it, but I'm tough, too. I get through and get over, everything and anything. That said, the truth is my soul was crushed on the edge of imminent heartbreaking loss. This dog had been a 24/7/365 proposition for me over the past fourteen years and a day.

Most of that time I'd been preparing – at least intellectually – for this day.

For the briefest instant I couldn't imagine life after this day.

The afternoon wore on, and Mac never moved.

He had no interest in the breakfast he'd never finished – possibly a first – and no interest in dinner – definitely a first

– just shutting down, as Dr. E. called it. And with each passing minute, realizing that Jake might not make it home in time, I began agonizing over that bit of fresh emotionally-charged territory I hardly needed.

The thought of that, on top of everything else, was simply nothing less than horrific. Jake's rekindled day-to-day relationship with Mac upon returning home after college had been beautiful to watch. The memories of it will always be precious to me. The love between them was honest and joyful and warmed my heart every day. A daily gift for them and for me. If Jake were too late, if he didn't get home in time, we'd all be devastated.

Jake worked until five but walked into the family room at a little after four and without a word rushed over to Mac. The old dog raised his head, looked up at Jake, and made eye contact as was his habit. After a few seconds he laid his head down.

And died.

The truth is we were all so blown away at first we weren't sure what had happened.

Shocked to the core which so inadequately describes it. Kneeling down by the most remarkable old dog, feeling for pulse, Evan confirmed it.

"He's gone," he told us simply.

As unreal and sad as it was, I felt a relief; Mackie was at peace and at rest. And bringing to an end these last couple of weeks, when for the first time in the 14 preceding years his life had been so diminished that the dignity with which he'd always carried himself had been so unjustly compromised, succumbing to the aggregate assault of time which finally dimmed his sparkle and stole his zest for life, his strength and incomparable will to live it.

The old dog had fought the good fight and the fight mercifully had come to an end.

Yeah, Mac was just a dog.

But he was our family dog, the best I'd ever know and I'll always believe the finest hunk 'o dog I'll ever know.

Unquestionably the dog of my life.

A great guy that touched so many lives in so many wondrous ways that I'll go to my grave believing he indeed wasn't your average dog, but a canine spirit that graced the lives of his people with his loving presence.

The boys helped me take him to our vet.

I'll never forget Evan wrapping him up in the rug; respectfully, lovingly, and tenderly. How he picked Mac up so gently, almost reverently, and carried him out the family room slider, Mac's in and out all of his life, and loaded him into the bed of his pickup for the short drive.

Mac's last trip to the vet.

I drove over separately and met them at the clinic.

Our dear friends there would make the final arrangements.

Like everything else in life today, end of life for dogs is its own business. Products and options I should have expected, but didn't, or avoided thinking about until given no choice.

I was a buyer and ordered plaster casts of paw prints for the boys.

The ashes would come home to Lynne and me; they live in our family room on a shelf above our home entertainment gear. A simple wooden urn with an engraved message that's almost what I wanted when, numbed, spent and emotionally drained, I ordered it that afternoon, scribbling it on a pad.

MAC
The best of the best.
The dog of my life.

I'll never forget our vet's reaction when she joined us at his side on the rug in a lower level of the clinic I'd never seen before.

She wept over him.

We all did.

The next day, like it or not, Lynne and I had family business out of town.

Life goes on, of course, and the day trip almost helped us not think about Mac every minute, but not quite. We were shocked but not shocked at all; this day had been in the making for a long time. Despite that, finding a way to accept the last new normal couldn't have seemed more out of reach. When we returned home, a gorgeous flower arrangement was waiting for us.

From our vet.

It was such a sweet and thoughtful and touching gesture and so like Dr. E.

And made us all cry, again.

ONE OF MAC'S LAST PICTURES.

CHAPTER TEN
The New Normal

From the *Better to have loved and lost* file I'll say that it's yet another old cliché that earned its stature for its time-tested truth. Getting over Mac hasn't been easy, and nearly a year later, while every day is no longer an issue there still are moments. It's fitting; getting over the old dog has been every bit as hard as I feared it might.

And you know what? I feel lucky for it. Blessed by it. I loved Bonnie. I loved Dapper maybe even more. I loved Ozzie in spite of himself. But Mac was a dog I loved for a friendship and kinship I never would have believed possible. A loving spirit leaving indelible paw prints in the hearts of our family. To me, a rare and precious gift.

I never thought I could live without a dog. Unthinkable. My house is empty without one. Too quiet. I miss the hassle, the mess, the goofy and cartoony. A true friend and pure spirit, loving and accepting me unconditionally. I can't say never, but can't yet imagine ever.

The best way to define the dog universe is that it's ginormous.

In the U.S., more than 43,346,000 households own dogs.

Just over 78 million dogs of all shapes, sizes, personalities and persuasion.

Mac was just one of them. But Mac was my dog.

As my best friend suggested when I began writing his story, it has been both therapeutic and acutely painful at times. The therapy is a good thing. I expected that. Writing has helped, another reason I love what I do. From the Tribute Post six days after Mac died, "The Old Dog's Final Gifts", included with a few others at the end of the book, it helps, in a wondrous way, somehow making him feel a little bit closer. Refreshing the memories like a personal hedge against them fading to almost forgotten.

I don't know if it's the nature of life or the chemistry of memory, but I'd like to fight that loss if I can. I'd like to prevent time from stealing that from me. If the price is occasional weepiness, I'll take pay that price and accept those teary moments as a gift, and cling fiercely to them. Far more devastating and worthy of tears is the thought of becoming so numbed by time that I no longer feel all that I feel which summons those tears.

Mac deserves to be remembered and not forgotten.

The first days were predictably horrific.

Our hearts were shattered, raw and exposed to a finality that was inarguable and undeniable but simultaneously unacceptable. We had to accept it, but in the moment, just couldn't.

Lynne summed it up, again and again and again.

I just can't believe he's gone   I really just can't believe it.

Our home was impossibly quiet and the silence screamed Mac's absence.

Every day was full of reminders that brought it all back. As Mac's primary caregiver my day had been full of the daily chores, food, water, meds, taking him in and out, trips to the vet, and time together.

Meds and medical items that had occupied the top of microwave in the kitchen for years.

I gathered them up, discarded what had no value, and donated the rest to our vet's clinic.

His harness and leash hang as they had all those years in our mudroom. They still do.

The *bag of bags* we used for walks is still hanging next to them, too. I'm still discovering, in every coat and jacket I own, a plastic bag or two. I never left home without a couple of bags, as they were as much a part of me as my wallet and cell phone. Mac's kennel is still in the corner of our family room. I never think of taking it down.

My house now is full of all the places he used to be.

My peripheral vision plays tricks on me but not as often.

Thinking I saw him out of the corner of my eye, Mac napping in one of his favorite spots, or just disappearing around a corner, as if he was the next room.

I still leave the house thinking about making sure Mac is where he should be and closing-up where he'd explore if we didn't.

I still come home, especially from the gym in the morning, and am shocked that he isn't there. Unsure whether to be embarrassed or grateful for it. Both, I guess.

What's left are the odd reminders; like the carpet stains from years of scary and irksome adventures. God, I'd love another adventure or two.

No longer does he finish breakfast or dinner and come over and burp in my face.

Lynne no longer complains when, after a drink of water, he shared it with a wet muzzle dripping over her.

Patches of grass that fell victim to his daily watering are filling in, and getting over it.

The old towels in the mudroom and on top of kennel, used to dry him out after going outside when it rained, no longer have to be washed periodically.

His huge English Lab head will never fit perfectly in my hand again. Now I settle for the portrait in a frame on the table and pat the top because it's the next best thing.

Memories come at odd times. Some are sad, other touchingly sweet.

I'll always marvel at what Labs allow small children to do: Pretty much everything without complaint or objection, and countless times I was astounded that Mac never once drew the line with them. I wouldn't have blamed him, but it was never a factor. He understood that these often wild little people meant no harm, and indulged them accordingly as a matter of course. Some of our best pictures are of Mac in the back yard with little ones lying atop.

All of the grandkids met Mac relatively late in his life and as a mature dog he was happy to let them have their way. He was happy for the attention. The youngest, twins just a year and a half-old old when he died, never fail to point to his picture. They didn't know him for long, but old guy sure made a lasting impression.

So many insignificant little things that together comprised the fabric of our lives together, banished to live with all our other memories of past days, lives and loves. We loved Mac not as much for the doggone good ole' dog he was, but for the true friend he was. For the handsome, unwaveringly loyal, cute and cuddly 110 lbs lapdog, too, because, while I'd swear he was some kind of evolved pooch on some level I'll never understand, he was also pure dog in all the best ways.

Friends and loved ones are so hard to say goodbye to. Their absence felt so keenly.

And so hard to get over. Countless times I wondered why he was so hard to get over.

Finally, many months later, I finally figured it out.

It wasn't the dog I'd lost, but the friend I'd lost.

In a lifetime with enough living and loving and losing, at a point to have Medicare snugly in my sights, and with more than my fair share of wonderful and true friends, Mac may have been the best friend I ever had. I say this making no apology or offering any explanation to my two-legged friends who might take offense, but think about it.

Mac accepted me in spite of me and forgave my numerous shortcomings that, I admit without hesitation, I also possess more than a fair share of. To Lynne's credit, she's put up with a lot, albeit not always quietly or without protest. Turning deaf ears, fairly, to my lame excuse of being a *slow learner*.

Mac on the other hand didn't see anything but perfection in me.

He didn't think that I ate too much.

Or suggested that I drink too much.

If I lost it when the Cardinals couldn't hit or blew a late lead, or overreacted to the Ducks missing an open field tackle or the Niners making a fatal stumble that cost them dearly, or was morally outraged when the umps or officials got it *totally wrong*, when I behaved like a child and not a grown man, none of that diminished me in any way to him.

No if's, and's or but's behind Mac's trademark and feverishly lavish doggie kisses that he'd bestow at the drop of a milk bone; it was pure, unadulterated love. Whether we deserve it that day, or any other day, it's simply their way. Like my vet had said to me more than once, what a world it would be if that it were our way. Our furry four-legged friends are love machines, accepting and forgiving love machines.

How lucky for us there's precious little we can do to talk them out of it.

And what does that tell us?

What can it teach us?

Baseball is ultimately a humbling game, full of the cruelty of repeated failure.

Good dogs are humbling in a different way. Lovingly reminding us of our largesse.

Putting us in our proper place without ever leaving theirs.

Mac had an odd puppyhood; surgeries trumped romping.

The Labrador retriever that couldn't and wouldn't retrieve.

He never learned to swim and in God's Country missed out on hikes.

We didn't do dog parks, feared other dogs being too playful and putting his joints at risk.

Doggie friends were limited to those we encountered on walks or at the vet.

He was never a car dog, because he couldn't get comfortable.

Our efforts to control his weight, so essential to give his

mechanically reconstructed hips, knees and elbows a fighting chance, left us perpetually guilty of starving him and despite that, the last years of inactivity put some of those lost pounds back. Still, he made do with what he got, ate every bit of the broccoli added to skinny rations to try and fill up his tummy, never complaining or begging, just gratefully being.

He loved his life and most of all he loved the people in his life, accepting whatever he had with the most wonderful dog's smile I've ever known.

Mac accepted his life and made the most of every day, joyfully and without complaint.

I wish I could say the same about me.

Unless he was eating, he was never too busy.

Treating everyone he met like a long lost friend, and greeting everyone he knew like his very best friend. Losing *that* kind of friend, that's what has made Mac so hard to get over. Because on some level I knew that, if you're lucky, you have that kind of friend once in your life, two or four-legged, but maybe not more than one. So the loss looms larger, not for the individual loss but for a richness and fullness that may not ever return.

Accept and forgive, live and love, and make every day and everyone count.

For as long as we can and as completely and selflessly as we can.

Mac, my beloved old dog sure had a few new tricks in him.

I'll thank him for the rest of my life for sharing them with me.

Paw Prints In My Heart

The house is still empty, and the hole in our hearts remains unfilled.

But the tears do stop and the heart finally stops aching.

Am I done as a dog owner? I hope not but I might be.

I greet every dog I see and enjoy my grand puppy when she visits.

The good memories, the sweetest ones, are thriving.

I'm thankful for having a dog I could call *the dog of my life*.

And thank you, Mac, for allowing me that great privilege.

Blog Posts about Mac

The Old Dog is 12 Years Old Today
June 13, 2011

Greetings from Portland, Oregon—MAC, the wonder lab, turns twelve today, seventy-five by my calculations in human years. It's quite an accomplishment because on the eve of his first birthday, the pick of the litter from a North American show champion, there were doubts he'd make it past two or three.

MAC at 12 years-old

We learned the adorable black puppy that captured our hearts was a veterinary orthopedic disaster. We thought he had a bad leg, but it turned out that all four legs, all his joints, had issues. Our choice was to do the unthinkable or do the unthinkable.

So, believing he could have an acceptable quality of life, we embarked on a program to 'fix' him. That meant five leg surgeries over the next two years. A bout with cancer, and other assorted other life-threatening events followed over the years, but for all of it, he's still smiling.

Paw Prints In My Heart

MAC is the happiest dog I've ever known, and he makes me laugh every day.

Smiling on a sunny day on the deck, one of his favorite spots.

He loves everyone he meets, routinely winning over even the non-dog lovers among us with a smile and direct eye contact.

For all the medical adventures, the physical limitations imposed by high-tech metallic devices is all his joints, and the daily gymnastics his 'mom and dad' accept as normal, none of it has in any way affected his spirit and love of life.

There's a lesson in it for all of us.

I've had dogs my whole life and loved every one, but this one was a gift, albeit an expensive one. We can only hope to have his quality of health care when our time comes.

His lifetime vet tab equals freshman and sophomore years at the U of O, no kidding.

Between his monthly Adequan injections, daily doses of Rimadyl for his arthritis, and a diet of the lowest-fat dog food made, sold only by veterinarians, of course, to keep his weight under a hundred, around about a hundred and fifty bucks a month when he's healthy.

A bargain because he's my best friend and writing partner, and cheaper than a therapist.

Our morning walks around the block are shorter now, and a lot slower. His muzzle is whiter than ever, and white hairs have invaded his massive black body from his paws to his eye brows. Most Sunday morning he still holds court at the Raleigh Hills Starbucks for a cadre of 'friends' – dog lovers and non-dog lovers he's won over – but we drive him now, the walk is too much.

Even as a canine senior citizen, I still consider him "the best looking male in the family" and no one argues the point.

Recently, my sister-in-law's family lost their beloved, Daisy, and my daughter's family had to say goodbye her wonderful kitty, Mabilis. There is no escaping these events that are unimaginable when a new puppy or kitten joins the family. They tear at our hearts.

I've been through it many times and hoped my words helped them in some small way.

Knowing, as I offered them, that, inevitably, my time is coming, as it does for all of us.

And that MAC may be the one I never quite get over.

I've already immortalized MAC in The Old Dog's New Trick. If you've read the second installment of The Mirano Trilogy, he inspired "Weller" and that's him on the cover.

But tonight we're celebrating his birthday, and he gets a special birthday dinner.

A half-pound Kobe beef burger from Trader Joe's, the fat and calories be damned.

And tomorrow I'll re-order his Rimadyl and Adequan.

Happy Birthday, Mackie!

Post 100: Happy Birthday to the Old Dog
June 12, 2012

*Greetings from Portland, Oregon—I'm a lucky dog guy.
Given the medical plight revealed at his first birthday,
"Mac", my 13 year-old Lab, has lived a wonderful and
improbably long life. That miracle came courtesy of lots of
love, dollars, and work; and was worth all of it. Even as a
puppy, I knew he was the dog of my life.*

*A lifetime of jumping through veterinary hoops has
made him the most expensive Man's Best Friend I'll ever
know. Joint issues, hips, knees and elbows, always limited
him physically; turning him into the Labrador retriever
who can't retrieve.*

*Half a dozen major surgeries and not only did he never
once complain, it couldn't change his love of people and his
trust of life, or dim the ever-present smile on his face that
never fails to bring one to mine.*

*Like I said, I'm lucky and know it. No dog ever loved his
people more, and was more loved.*

Andrew Hessel

So, for the occasions of my 100th Post, my fourth novel, 10,000 unique visitors to the website, and Mac's birthday to align together at this moment, well, somehow it seems just right.

Every bit the old dog now, he sleeps most of the day, can't hear a lick, and we only get flashes, brief glimpses of puppyhood from time to time, usually at breakfast and dinner. He still demands his morning walk, and although it can't get much slower or shorter I'm sure it will. But we'll never quit taking them, even if I have to improvise a cart of some kind if it comes to that.

My writing partner and best friend, my wife understands when I say that, and the inspiration for Old Dog Publishing and the character, Weller, a favorite of mine from The Old Dog's New Trick.

Happy 13th Birthday, old guy!

From everyone that loves you, and that's pretty much anyone that ever met you.

Blackstrap Molasses and other Old Dog Folk Remedies
September 4, 2012

Greetings from Portland, Oregon—At thirteen, Mac, my old lab Mac has already outlived expectations. Slowing down and graying up doesn't quite cover it these days. I've had dogs all my life, but never really understand how slow he could get, or how gray, but he's still smiling, as am I. That's all that matters these days.

What follows isn't exactly a recommendation, but I'm throwing it out there for anyone with an old dog that is having a harder and harder time getting around.

I think it's helping, but first a little context.

As a rule, I'm not a holistic dude, although I'd like to consider myself open-minded when it comes to medical care, especially when it comes to my dog. Meaning: I'll try anything.

And, in that spirit, I have tried just about everything.

After five leg surgeries, hips, knees and elbows, a cancer surgery and a few other medical emergencies, I'm not dog-whistlin' Dixie.

Presently, in addition to a special diet (the lowest fat dog food on the market with cooked broccoli on top to give him a full tummy without calories) Mac gets 100mg of Rimadyl with each meal. And, after five years of regular Adequan injections, we're bumping up the schedule to every three weeks from four weeks, and hoping that helps.

Still, looking for something else, I stumbled across

something on a blog about old dogs and blackstrap molasses. I had no idea what that was, but learned it's what's left after the maximum extraction from sugar, after boiling it three times. Thank you, Wikipedia.

Apparently, a dose on top of food yielded results for some creaky old dogs. That was all I had to hear and I was off to the store. It's readily available. I first tried the organic; a little thicker than the non-organic, and predictably more expensive. I switched to the regular after the first bottle and see no difference.

My vet thinks I'm a little nutty and that's an undeniable fact.

After six weeks or so, I think it might be helping.

Still slow ... as, well, molasses – but less limping, so I'm sticking with it.

The Old Dog Hobbles to Fourteen
June 14, 2013

Greetings from Portland, Oregon–Yesterday we celebrated Mac's 14th birthday. His morning prednisone hidden in a "peanut butter breadie-ball" illustrates how "on his last legs" now has literal and figurative meaning. We've been lucky – all the metal in his hips, knees and elbows gave him more time than we ever expected.

=The truth is, for all the surgeries that began when he was one, and the medication, emergencies, special diet and a lifetime medical tab we laughingly think of as his freshman and sophomore years at the U of O, I'm astounded by how truly grateful I am for it.

This is the dog I know I'll never get over, but for the many tears already shed, and all of those sure to come, I wouldn't have traded any of it.

The dog of your life comes but once and only if you're very, very lucky. I certainly have been.

He's been nothing short of a gift that has made me laugh every day and still does.

We know we're in the last days of what my vet calls his 'sunset years' but the fact is we've been in that place for quite some time. My wonderful old lab has been declining since Halloween and along the way we've had a fair number of crises.

The morning walks Mac and I took each day of his life (other than during the eight-week recuperation periods following each of his five leg surgeries) came to a halt this past January.

I miss 'em. Mac loved them so, he lived for his walks. But as is his way and the stoic nature of the breed, never complained when they ended. As always, he seemed to understand and accept the physical limitations that he's lived with since puppyhood.

This is the Labrador retriever that was never actually quite able to retrieve ... hard to do when you're operating on elbows that, virtually without cartilage, are essentially bone-on-bone.

The wonder of it, he's still smiling and as long as he's happy to be around, and can still hobble around, we'll do whatever it takes to keep him comfortable and enjoy each day.

Given Mac's special needs and my role as primary doggie caregiver, I have witnessed, in a way I never did with my previous dogs, the transition from mature to senior to elderly. I never knew a dog once black as night could get so gray. By the way, the photo is recent, and compared to ones on my website or that I use in online profiles with a similar pose, you'll get a sense of just how much grayer he is today.

For those that don't know, it's Mac on the cover of my second novel, The Old Dog's New Trick. He inspired the title, and Weller, an old lab that plays an important role in the story, and returned in Imperfect Resolution, the final installment of The Mirano Trilogy, and will make another appearance in the new Cups Drayton crime thriller arriving next year.

Paw Prints In My Heart

You could say I've immortalized the old dog.
A friendly reminder for all you dog lovers out there:
Enjoy the time.

Andrew Hessel

The Old Dog's Final Gifts
June 19, 2013

Greetings from Portland, Oregon –

A day after turning 14, hours after writing his birthday post, my beloved lab, Mac, passed. We're devastated. Long fearing the one I'd never get over, now I'll find out. For all the loss and sadness, even at the end he was the best of the best, leaving after giving us two amazing gifts.

Saying goodbye is the hardest part; the shocking and soul-crushing finality of the inevitable. After I tell the story, with selected pics from puppy to mature to senior to elderly, there are links to four past posts about a dog that was my true friend and a beloved family member.

The tipping point was quality of life. While prednisone gave us a few bonus weeks, last Friday the quality was gone. As were his rear legs, his strength and an ever-present sparkle in his eyes and smile. Lynne and I knew he'd let us know and he surely did. Mid-morning last Friday I knew the end had come, and made "the call" to our vet; she'd make a house call at 7 pm.

June 13 1999 to June 14 2013. He'd lived a doggone good dog's life. Working from home most of those years, we'd spent most every day together. Mac was my writing partner and Old Dog Publishing was more than just a name to me.

I alerted our three sons that it was time to say goodbye. As the afternoon wore on, Mac slept. Weaker and weaker still, with no interest in anything, even food and that was a first. So unlike my 100+lb. English Lab that was truly the densest hunk 'o dog I've ever known and an eating machine. The last six years we'd fed him the lowest fat dog food we could buy garnished with a half of pound of broccoli so he'd feel full without calories and ease the burden on his legs.

Waiting for my boys, the hours passed glacially. I feared our youngest son that had grown up with Mac, adored him and always lived with him might not make it in time. Meanwhile, inching closer to the grim scene when our vet arrived I tried not thinking about it, and failed miserably.

Jake got home a little after four pm and went straight to Mac. The old dog looked up and saw him, and then, having seen him, let go, stopped breathing and died peacefully.

Just like that it was over. Mac was gone, but on his terms, after first giving us two precious gifts.

First, thankfully, he'd waited for Jake. And then, he spared us having to put him down.

You know, our vet wept when we took him in late Friday afternoon, and she sent flowers to the house on Saturday. I took it as heartfelt acknowledgement of a rock star patient that was a legend in their clinic. For his extraordinary medical history, he'd always loved going to the vet ... and we went a lot. He loved the people there and they loved him. When he stayed over, for him it almost like going to Camp.

On Sunday, Father's Day while wonderful was painfully

different.

More than missed, Mac's absence was ever-present. The silence in our house is deafening.

With our family gathered for our Father's Day BBQ, I made this toast:

"Lynne asked me if I could make it through a toast to Mac without crying.

I answered, "Probably ... not." Adding, "You know me, how could I? Of course, I can't."

So, rather than winging it and losing it, I wrote it so I'd say what I need to say.

About Skye Mac of Oregon, his never-used AKC name: He was Mac; Mackie; my baby boy, my fourth son; my bionic lab.

The best-looking man in our family and the handsomest lab face I ever saw.

Dogs are great companions. A few are irreplaceable friends. He truly was.

Mac liked dogs but loved people. Everyone. And if you think about it, he had a complex relationship with each of you, something that was just between the two of you. In his way, he was everyone's best friend, and while he was with you knew it was true.

He was the purest, sweetest, goodest and bestest dog of all, and as smart as they come. Before losing his hearing, I'd lost track of how many words he knew. We'd often tell him to meet us on Mommy's deck or the patio, and he'd go out the family room slider, wind his way through the yard to the far side of the house and be waiting for us when we arrived. With a smile on his face.

Mac was also the ultimate stoic.

Five leg surgeries and a bout with cancer couldn't change his personality or dim his love and trust of life.

The old dog had always accepted his physical limitations happily because it's all he knew and all he really wanted was to be with us.

He had the greatest doggie smile I've ever seen, unfailingly made me laugh every day and was truly a terminal licker-kisser. He sure put that massive tongue to good use.

Mac was the dog of my life.

Sometimes it's hard to know what you can believe in. But I do believe in dog heaven, and I think he's just been elected president of the neighborhood up there. He's surrounded by great dogs, running like he never could, and enjoying the all-you-can-eat doggie buffet sans broccoli.

This is a toast to Mac: It was an honor and my privilege.

I know just how lucky I was that for 14 years you were ours. I'll never forget you."

Acknowledgements

I've reached a point in life where I no longer consider even the smallest acts of kindness to be small things and offer thanks to generous family members and friends for their help.

My wife, Lynne, as always, has supported my efforts through five books and a journey she never signed on for, and has been an indispensable first reader and de facto editor. This one was a particular challenge, as the subject matter hit so close to home during a time when we struggled mightily with broken hearts to bear the loss of a dear friend, Mac. Despite all of that, she was, again, a tireless cheerleader and patiently allowed me her honest feedback. I am forever in her debt and thankful for so many things I fear I'll never adequately repay.

My dear friend and pro bono editor, Ken Courian, again waded through the manuscript and with a smile endured everything from misplaced commas to others MIA; no shortage of discrepancies and redundancies, and faithfully pointed out opportunities to improve the narrative in ways both large and small. His wife Terri again lent a hand with food, drink and good cheer as we worked through it together and I am truly thankful.

Sincere thanks to my closest friend, and brother by different mothers, Ken Graham, for his compassion during hard times and for urging me to write this story at the right time for the right reasons. I never believed I'd know people who would go as far as Lynne and I did for their four-legged pals, but Ken and his wife Kris, have done that and possibly even more.

My sons, Jake, Evan and Aaron, offered memories of Mac that were important elements to the story, and reminded me of still others. Diane Minears and Eddie Ward again generously read the early manuscript.

My sister, Susan T. Hessel, again prepared the manuscript for publication and, incredibly, created the cover when my designer was unable to. Amazingly, as she has been all our lives, Sue is there for me, cheerfully doing whatever I ask and dismissing my fits of frustration, panic and self-inflicted madness to make it possible to turn a dream into a book. I may have to reconsider the infamous yo-yo and return it to her if I could only find it.

To all of us that love dogs for the companionship and friendship they offer and the warmth and laughter they add to even the longest days and most severely bruised hearts, thanks for reading. You're an essential part of a story that's bigger than Mac and me, because it's part of all of us.

Enjoy a Free Preview
of
The Old Dog's New Trick

If you enjoyed *Paw Prints in My Heart* and meeting Mac, the first three chapters of *The Old Dog's New Trick* follow. I invite you to meet *Weller,* the old black lab Mac inspired.

Old Dog is the second novel in the Cups Drayton Series, and Part Two of the Mirano Trilogy, which includes *Rush to Dawn, The Old Dog's New Trick* and *Imperfect Resolution.* I wrote them to be read as stand-alone novels or as a trilogy. Readers have enjoyed them in and out of order, but if your preference is to read in sequence, I wanted you to know.

A little about getting the books.

All of my books are available as Kindle eBooks through Amazon.

Paw Prints and *The Do-Over* – a Kiki Kinsler novel – are also available in paperback through www.amazon.com. The Cups Drayton Series is available in paperback through Publishers Graphics, **www.pubgraphics.com.**

For links and to learn more please visit my website: www.pleasereadmybookbeforeidie.com

If you chuckled at my web address, know that every day it's closer to the truth, so please hurry and visit while I'm still waking up on the right side of the grass.

—Andrew

And now a preview of *The Old Dog's New Trick*:

*W*hen Mira Mirano, the first Lady Don, succeeded her father as head of the powerful Mirano crime family, she'd earned the right.

Thanks to a brilliant mind and a staggering resume of flawless assassinations.

Respected – and feared - she had been unopposed. No one even considered a challenge.

Under her leadership, she led The Family to new heights, expanding their reach, power and wealth by pioneering innovative new businesses and techniques while strengthening and legitimizing core businesses.

By every measure, she was the right woman for the job and the times.

Then Cups Drayton costs her a key business partner, brings the family under the federal microscope and interrupts a perfect plan.

Mira has never tasted defeat.

And not a woman to take it quietly.

Outraged and with her pride wounded, she viciously strikes back, launching a multi-faceted character assassination campaign against Chief of Detectives Elliot Rose, Cups closest friend.

As part of a plan to lure Cups to his death, Rose is abducted, secreted in a remote place few even know exists and where no one would ever imagine looking. Mira directs Raul Mendoza, the new Family assassin whose weapon of choice is as historically elegant as it is deadly and cold, to finish all of them off.

The FBI's top forensic analyst, Allan Goldman, returns in Old Dog, this time bringing new technology and tools to Oregon.

From the volcanic mountains of the High Cascades of Central Oregon to the streets and city parks of Portland, good and evil battle to the death. Weller, an orphaned old lab who adopts himself into Cups new family, proves that even old dogs have a trick or two left.

If Cups is to prevail, he'll need every one of them.

Chapter 1

As the man turned the key to open the door to his condo the cell phone in his shirt pocket vibrated. He was no stranger to odd hours and ambitious travel schedules, but a deep fatigue weighed heavily. Weather delays in San Francisco resulted in an arrival at Sea-Tac hours later than planned. At least the assignment, as always, had been flawlessly performed. No surprises and surgically precise, he never failed. It was his custom, his trademark, and he took justifiable pride knowing he was the best of the best. Closing the door behind him, he glanced at Caller ID.

WITHHELD – NO DATA

"Yes."

"Are you home?" The woman asked.

"I've just arrived."

"The timing for this isn't ideal, I know, but I have another assignment: A clean-up which can't wait, in Mexico City. There is a situation we can't allow to become a risk; dealing with it eliminates that possibility. Can you do this for me? I'll text you details."

"Of course, I'll leave right away."

"Raul, I appreciate this … and you."

"I know. Thank you."

"One last thing, I want you to …" Mira Mirano seemed to struggle finding the words, and failing to do so fell silent.

"Yes?"

"…Have a safe and successful trip."

"Always."

Not long after, showered and in fresh clothes, he was back in the air and on his way.

Raul Mendoza slept well on planes, possessing the uncanny, soldier-like ability to sleep whenever he could. The stepson of Artie Mirano's cousin who served as the Family's liaison to the Mexican drug cartels, he had grown up in Mexico City. Now the Family's enforcer, problem solver and clean-up specialist, Raul spoke fluent Spanish and looked like a successful Latin American businessman. In a light gray summer suit, black silk shirt, and a solid gold chain around his neck that, by Mexican standards, was understatedly elegant. His alligator attaché case contained a few files, props for effect. Despite flying privately and with customs agents well rewarded to look the other way, he traveled this time without a gun. He rarely needed one.

It wasn't his preferred tool.

Raul Mendoza used the garrote almost exclusively. He loved its silence. He also loved the feel of razor-sharp wire effortlessly biting into flesh as if it had a mind of its own, possessed by an ancient spirit guiding it along on a path to sever the vocal cords and jugular before decapitating the often unsuspecting target if given free reign.

No sound and no ballistics. Forensics left little trace.

Raul was a pro. Long Mira's counterpart in Mexico, she had summoned him to Seattle to take her place when she assumed control of The Family. She respected his skill above all others and needed a personal assassin she could trust unequivocally. Despite their history – or perhaps because of it – Raul was her man.

They were the same age and had met as children at Family gatherings and vacations in Mexico and Seattle, spending time together as playmates, and, later, exploring their simultaneous adolescent sexual yearnings together. Mira was his first and she was his teacher, losing her virginity a year earlier at thirteen to her father's bodyguard who paid the steepest of prices when his transgression was discovered. Mira, in no way scarred by it, embraced her sexuality from the first moment she grasped the commanding power her beauty and brains gave her over men.

"Where did you *learn* these things?" Raul had asked with his head cradled between her breasts. He was trying to catch his breath after the first time but caring little if he did.

"I was born to it," she joked, stroking his hair tenderly. "*My* teacher marveled at my innate skill. He praised what he called the rare ability to suck a tennis ball through a garden hose."

"Doubtful," he chided, "that's just polite exaggeration from a *very* grateful older man, I'm sure." Raul said this in a voice playfully taunting, leaving no doubt he was daring her to prove him wrong.

Mira rolled out from under him, turned him over and said in a voice huskier than any girl her age had a right to, "I'll let you judge for yourself." She went right to work to prove her point.

And did.

In their early twenties, the two young people completed

their final training together. Both excelled under the aging but watchful eyes of esteemed Family killers they were being groomed to succeed. Final exams were two assignments needing a team to meet challenges requiring theater as well as cold efficiency. Given the exacting standards and high degree of difficulty, passing them handily earned admiration and reward rare at comparatively young ages.

For Raul, returning home to Mexico City always elicited the same response: Fascination and repulsion with the city built by the Aztecs in 1325 and once known as Tenochtitlan. The Spanish Explorer Hernan Cortes arrived in 1519, two years before his siege of the city ended Montezuma's rule and changed both the nation and Latin America forever. Its population then was just over half a million. Today it has grown to nearly twenty million, becoming one of the half dozen largest cities on earth.

Mexico City is a city of issues. Perhaps no city is as singularly, if disproportionately, prominent in every phase of its country's affairs. It is a gargantuan city, with a GDP of nearly half a trillion dollars, vividly showcasing the harsh and bitter contrasts between the haves and the have-nots. Almost obscene wealth of the privileged juxtaposed by millions doomed to inescapable abject poverty. A rich, historic culture classically apparent in parks and museums, flanked by the best worst case example of the most hideous inequities of 21st Century urban life.

Even at 7349 feet above sea level, the humidity in Mexico City can be oppressive much of the year. High temperatures in what's known as the Valley of Mexico are mitigated and don't typically rise out of the eighties, but that far south humidity abides. Surrounded by mountains, thermal inversions are quite common and with high altitude already compromising the amount of oxygen in the atmosphere, air quality is some of the worst anywhere. Eight million cars on the road conspire to seal the deal creating staggering pollution levels and attending respiratory problems.

"We'll be landing shortly," the flight attendant advised, gently resting her hand on his shoulder and rousing him from a catnap. "Would you like anything?" She asked hopefully.

She'd been carefully considering the handsome man who was her only passenger. Tall and broad shouldered without an ounce of fat, Raul wore his thick, longish black hair swept back with impressive sideburns and a goatee. Everything pointed to the fact that he was rich, too. She'd taken note of the elegantly tailored suit and the most beautiful calfskin loafers she'd ever seen; this was a passenger she wanted to get to know. Intelligent, polite and refined, he spoke beautiful English without an accent, perhaps the faintest trace of one. Good looking and well mannered, a far more attractive candidate than the old coots she typically served on these private charters, but he'd given her no opportunity. Undeterred, she shifted to a back-up plan.

"Nothing, but thank you for inquiring," he smiled politely.

He knew she'd been puzzled that he hadn't left his seat the entire flight, never using the lavatory or touching a cup or glass. Just before landing he'd discreetly wipe the armrests with a cloth from his attaché, insuring that there would be no trace of him. He traveled without luggage and his attaché lay on the vacant seat next to him.

"Will you be in Mexico City long?" she asked with an

invitingly coquettish tilt of her head designed to communicate that she was interested and available, "I have two days …"

A pretty girl, he thought, eyeing her arresting and ably displayed assets. A shame I don't.

"Sadly, not this time," seeing disappointment which abated when he added, "but I'd very much like your number for next time," he was pleased but not at all surprised when a folded page of note paper clenched tightly in her hand appeared. Well aware of the effect he had on women, especially impressionable young and highly ambitious ones, Raul had expected it.

Breezing through customs to a black late model Volvo sedan waiting in the parking lot of the charter facility, Raul climbed into the front seat and in thirty minutes was driving down Mexico City's most famous and impressive boulevard, *Paseo de la Reforma,* ordered built by Emperor Maximilian I in 1860 during the Second Mexican Empire. It was originally called *The Empress's Avenue,* in honor of Empress Carlota, and cut a straight-as-a- preacher twelve-mile diagonal swath across the city. *La Reforma,* reminiscent of many of Europe's great boulevards, links Chapultepec Park and Castle with the historic old city's financial and business center as well as other districts and ultimately newer commercial centers. *La Reforma* provides easy access – except on Sunday when it is closed to vehicular traffic – to newer, more recently developed areas like Santa Fe, home to *Centro Comercial Santa Fe,* the largest mall in Mexico.

Despite its prominence, historical importance and the natural attraction *La Reforma* has always held for the upscale and exclusive residential neighborhoods it spawned, late in the Twentieth Century many banks were wooed away to the newer, trendy areas. A move a few old school conservatives viewed with amusement, staunchly resisting progress and ultimately being proven correct. The sprawl made travel difficult and resulted in high vacancies, troubled commercial mortgages and dashed expectations.

Unimpressed, *Banco Universal* had held fast and refused to take the bait. As a result, the bank increased its stature and leadership position and ultimately exploited its advantage by gobbling up troubled leases and capitalizing upon them during a subsequent revival and boom. Juan Borbon, The Family's man inside the bank, lived in *El Sol,* a prestigious glass and chrome high rise within easy walking distance of the bank.

Juan Borbon had been useful to Mira but was now an unacceptable liability.

The large lobby of *El Sol* opened into a lushly landscaped atrium rising up forty-nine floors with cascading waterfalls on each side, ringed by upscale shops and eateries, only a few of which were open at this early hour. Nonetheless, the smell of strong, Mexican coffee was already in evidence. *El Sol* was a planned, self-contained community conceived for only the wealthiest and most influential, with commercial offices on the next half dozen floors and preposterously expensive apartments on the next forty floors. It was rumored that Carlos Slim, Mexico's wealthiest man and one of the world's most powerful, retained the entire top floor for a penthouse he used when in Mexico City.

Raul walked with purpose, unhurried, to the express elevators that would take him to Juan Borbon's apartment. Adjacent to the impressive bank of elevators was an information desk manned by an older, balding man who appeared to be as wide as he was tall. Even a casual glance from a distance told Raul what he needed to know; the old man was uncomfortable and sweating although the temperature inside was a never varying 72 degrees. Drinking from an oversized mug, his mouth full of hard-crusted breakfast rolls, it was clear that only an act of war would prompt him to action, and maybe not even that.

"*Buenas Dias,*" Raul said softly, making sure the old man saw the key card in his hand. .

"*Buenas Dias, señor,*" he replied, his eyes looking down in deference as the visitor disappeared inside the elevator that, after swiping his key card, began its ascent. When the doors opened on the thirty-eighth floor, Raul peeked out, gazing to his left and right before exiting. Seeing no one, he paused to open his attaché and removed three items: He put on disposable booties like carpet cleaners leave their customers to walk on wet carpet and a pair of rubber dishwashing gloves. The garrote he slipped into his suit jacket pocket.

Outside the door of Apartment 38-A he stopped and listened. Hearing nothing, he opened the door and once inside coaxed it closed without making a sound, stopping again to listen.

He knew the importance of working quickly but also staying in control; avoiding too sudden movements in a target's home. Borbon was in the shower, Raul could hear him singing a song he recognized but couldn't name. Continuing down the hallway and into the bedroom he took up a position behind the bathroom door. This target had made it easy for him and he appreciated it.

It wouldn't be long.

A few minutes later he heard the water of the shower stop, the plumbing groaning in response and Raul almost laughed – even the nicest buildings weren't immune, suffering their own infrastructure quirks. Borbon was humming now. He began to blow-dry his hair but was interrupted by the telephone. Cursing softly, he turned off the dryer and opened the door.

From his suit pocket Raul removed his garrote.

In his mind it was the most elegant of weapons.

So old, so reliable, so familiar, and so at home in his hand; he became one with it.

He waited, hidden in darkness, until Borbon stepped past him. Without a sound, Raul sprang forward from behind and with a precise and polished move looped the wire around Borbon's neck, pulling back. He tightened the pressure with a remarkably fluid efficiency of movement, the result of years of practice perfecting his craft.

Borbon barely whimpered, uttering a sound so small and ineffectual Raul barely heard it. He loved the predictable reaction of every victim; hands flying in desperate panic to the wire, reacting to the pressure, fighting against it, throat filling with blood, struggling to breathe but unable to, no longer able to resist … at all … it ends.

Effortlessly cutting into flesh, the wire sings its silent Death Song.

Relaxing the pressure and removing the garrote with a graceful release of the left hand, Juan Borbon tumbled face forward into deep pile carpeting that would need to be replaced for the next tenant.

Gathering up Borbon's wallet, IPhone and laptop, Raul put them in his briefcase and quickly moved to the kitchen where he played the messages on Borbon's machine. There were three; one from his secretary reminding him of his ten o'clock. The next came from his wife checking in from Acapulco where she was vacationing with their children. The last, the call he had failed to answer, was from a young woman who frantically apologized for the night before and begged for another chance.

There would be no second chance.

The answering machine was old, and used a small micro cassette tape. Raul suspected the dead man had migrated voice mail to his IPhone but, because he took no unnecessary chances, removed the tiny cassette and tossed it into his attaché with the other items.

A quick search of files in Borbon's home office revealed nothing of what he had done for The Family. On his desk were a couple of family pictures of a heavy-set wife and adolescent children in wooden frames. Raul wondered why he had agreed to help Mira Mirano.

Most likely he needed the extra money.

It no longer mattered.

Borbon had evidently heeded the not-so-vague threats to avoid anything that would leave a trail. There was nothing here and it was doubtful there was anything in his office at the bank. Mira hadn't appeared concerned about that. She'd never even mentioned it.

Raul smiled, deeply satisfied with what had transpired. The hallway was still empty. At the elevators he pushed the Down button, removing his gloves and booties as he waited.

Raul checked his watch and smiled, he might be home for a mid-afternoon lunch.

Not bad, he thought, not bad at all.

Chapter 2

From the front porch of the ranch house the view to the West was more than impressive; it might have graced a jaw-dropping post card. The rugged, craggy peaks of the Three Sisters and Three Finger Jack rose imposingly in the distance. The day's bright sunlight was reflected off deep snow still crowning them with a thick white blanket beginning well below the tree line. A colder, wetter winter than usual had endowed Central Oregon with more precipitation than in years; dumping drenching valley rains and burying the mountains under near-record snows.

This late in spring, the generous snow pack remaining was more reminiscent of a winter wonderland than rapidly approaching summer, tenaciously resisting warming temperatures, and challenging the sunny days with a cheerful, confident defiance. Jubilant skiers were predicting the best summer ski season in memory, dreaming of roaring down the slopes on the Fourth of July in cut-offs, tee shirts and sunglasses. Old-timers were reminded of year 'round skiing when winter snows in the mountains successfully outlasted even the fiercest summer heat.

The woman wondered if this might be one of those years.

Reclining on a weathered but sturdy and well-maintained Adirondack sipping her morning coffee, she looked across a vast, forty-acre meadow stretching to the foothills. The screened in porch with a retractable awning and fire pit enabled her to enjoy the cedar deck comfortably in all weather, even mountain winters in Oregon.

She wasn't an outdoors woman; rather, a hardened city girl who'd grown up at hyper-speed in one of Seattle's most affluent northern suburbs. Despite easy access to breathtaking mountains and unforgettable beaches, she'd never had the time or interest in such pursuits. So very much her father's daughter; her life had always been business first, rarely allowing anything else – or *anyone* else – to matter. For most of her life the beauty of the natural world never engaged her – it was little more than scenic wallpaper. Her appreciation for it was passive and at arms-length.

But that was before.

So many things had changed in the last year or so; some subtle, others much less so but none more surprising than her evolving relationship with the natural world. She supposed it might simply be that beauty is harder to ignore when it smacks you in the face at every turn as it did her these days.

Whatever the explanation, she no longer took for granted what she once had, recognizing that people scrimped, saved and slaved all year to briefly visit the two places she now called home.

She divided her time between the villa on Sifnos, an enchanted but lesser known Greek Island in the Western Cyclades, and the high desert mountain retreat at Big Crescent Lake in the Oregon Cascades. Technology enabled her to effectively rule her criminal empire not unlike a software engineer telecommuting from Sun Valley to the Silicon Valley in her bathrobe.

Her respect for the beauty of the world surrounding her was in no way a new reverence for what she'd always dismissed as marginally relevant. It was more an acknowledgement and acceptance of how much she had come to value the calming respite it offered her.

The shocker was realizing she *needed* it – needed *anything*, she never had before.

As a woman who rose to absolute power in a once exclusively man's world, Mira Mirano had more than thrived, but vulnerability of any kind could never be shown or shared with anyone. Her enemies and rivals watched vigilantly for the slightest sign of weakness.

They wouldn't find any.

More than their equal, after meeting her it was clear that crossing her came with a price few were prepared to pay. She demanded loyalty, respect, absolute obedience and got it.

Raul had confirmed completion of the Mexico City assignment. He had never failed her, and never would. Unwavering fidelity from soldiers like Raul, assured her safety and their own.

A family of deer grazed leisurely in the meadow's thick grasses which were just beginning their annual transition from the vibrant spring green of new growth to a deeper, darker summer green before July and August scorched them a lifeless brown. In the farthest northwest corner of the meadow was a fair sized pond. She could see its calm blue waters glistening even at this distance. Lacing up her hiking boots and zipping a light fleece against the morning chill, she descended the steps off the deck and began walking up the trail to the pond.

The walk to the pond had become a daily ritual and led to a surprising new relationship. As she approached she saw the gander, the male Canada goose she'd named Wilson. Upon hearing his familiar call she couldn't help but smile. Even as a child Mira had never had a pet and wasn't sure a wild bird qualified as one despite the pleasant, if unlikely, companionship they provided each other.

Flocks of the large birds came and went throughout the year, filling the sky with their trademark V-formation. As months and seasons passed Wilson never left, remaining steadfastly by the pond. Mira traveled and was often away for weeks at a time, half expecting when she returned to find him gone but she never did. Puzzled, she wondered about it until discovering the decomposed carcass of what she believed to be his mate nearby, evidently the victim of a coyote or other predator.

Why did the gander stay? Why didn't he depart with the flock or join another?

Intrigued, she researched the Canada goose online, quickly becoming fascinated with what she learned was the second largest bird in North America. Males can weigh 25 pounds with impressive wingspans of more than six feet, only the swan is larger. The world population, constituted by more than half a dozen different species and up to 200 sub-species, is estimated at over five million.

Although indigenous to Northern Canada and Alaska, the Canada goose has been successfully introduced in Europe, Scandinavia, Asia and even New Zealand. They are amazing creatures of habit migrating thousands of miles, using landmarks and the stars, to return to the same places year after year.

Interesting stuff, mundane tidbits, but not the answer she sought.

That she found by first reading enthusiasts' Birding Blogs with anecdotal stories and lore and then turning to more scholarly works detailing the behavioral characteristics of the birds.

The Canada goose can live more than twenty years and mates for life; they demonstrate a devotion transcending expectations. As parents, loyalty to each other and their offspring – goslings – goes far beyond animal instinct to nurturing qualities that are decidedly more *human*. Common is the sight of geese with their goslings following in orderly procession, one parent in front, the other in back, guiding, guarding, protecting and teaching.

She learned that animal intelligence is often overestimated, hardly a surprise given the hopeful passion of pet owners and animal lovers. The surprise was finding the opposite is true with animals' *emotional* range. Its scope is missed, overlooked and commonly misunderstood.

One thing shocked her: Canada Geese exhibit an inarguably human capacity to *grieve*.

Dr. Konrad Lorenz, the Austrian Nobel Prize winning zoologist, animal psychologist and ornithologist, is considered to be the father of modern ethology; the study of instinctive animal behavior. Enchanted by the species, one sentence from one of his classic works, *The Year of the Greylag Goose*, summed up the behavioral similarities when grieving:

"Quite literally, a man, a dog, and a goose hang their heads, lose their appetites, and become indifferent to all stimuli emanating from the environment."

Soul-crushing life events overwhelm creatures of all kinds, not just human beings.

Mira found literally dozens of accounts of a goose grieving inconsolably for a lost mate. The story of a goose with a broken wing attempting to walk south during a fall migration as her gander circled above, at times dropping to earth to accompany her on foot. Geese, whose mates are shot by hunters and, although endangered, return to them, maintaining endless vigils in the most unlikely places such as freeway bridges over rivers in major cities. They are overpowered by their emotional bonds and ultimately meet the same mortal fate.

Reaching the pond Wilson honked excitedly in recognition of her arrival.

Mira was amused, as always, by the comically formal look which his black head and neck with the white *chinstrap* afforded him. Wilson had lost his mate and apparently seemed disinclined to seek another. Choosing instead to remain alone, separated from his flock, forlorn of all hope, in an unending state of solitary melancholy. His body seemed hunched over, as if weighted down by his sadness and grief, screeching his pitiful, sorrowful cry.

Despite such heart-rending mourning, it's not uncommon for geese to bond with people. Wilson appeared to genuinely enjoy Mira's visits; perhaps both woman and goose intuitively valued their most unexpected friendship and found solace in each other.

Mira didn't really understand love; love was beyond her

experience and capacity.

But she did understand loyalty, and *loss*; suffering not long ago the loss of the only man she'd ever cared about and had allowed to get close enough to mean *anything* to her. Deprived of a comfort and kinship she didn't expect to have again, her response was rage and resentment.

She knew she'd eventually get past it and make it right one day.

That day couldn't come soon enough.

She sat on a large boulder at the edge of the pond, eyes closed, the sun warm on her face, lost in her thoughts. Mira wasn't mourning and was in no way paralyzed to inaction by the hand fate had indifferently dealt her, but she did feel uncharacteristically listless and unfocused. Her passion for living had been cruelly ripped away, and she had no idea how to cope with it. For her a confusing and unfamiliar feeling; there had been days when she wondered if it was too much for her, if she could deal with it – or wanted to.

Now for the first time she knew she was finally coming out of it.

Wilson had approached without her knowledge and, startling her with a honk, was now only a few yards away. At such a close distance Mira could clearly see the grief in his somber countenance.

Grief the bird clung to, fiercely refusing to let it go, surrendering totally to it.

"Time, Wilson, time will heal us if we just get on with life," she said softly, chagrined as she reflected on her own words. "You know, Wilson, you can't take my advice, but *I* certainly can."

Rising to her feet and stretching, Mira Mirano felt a bit sheepish it had taken her so long to come to this. She of all people knew undirected anger in a vacuum was a pointless and self-indulgent dead-end. Fortunately, she had the perfect plan to put it all behind her once and for all.

Getting even she understood; vengeance was a sensible, proper and suitable response. It was past time to execute the plan. Once she did she'd begin to really live again. Walking back she felt better with each step and by the time she'd reached the cabin her spirits were soaring.

Tomorrow she'd be back in Greece.

In Oregon, all she'd planned would soon be underway.

Chapter 3

The reader board at *Burger Heaven* said: *Otherworldly burgers and more!*

Burger Heaven was crowded even late on Friday afternoon before the dinner rush. Local school kids were enjoying a three-day weekend courtesy of a Teacher In-Service day, so business was booming at the mall, Cineplex and nearby shops and eateries. Lines were steady and deep for *Heavenly Big-Guy Burgers,* spilling out the door of the wildly popular fast food sensation that in less than a year had *everybody* talking and their competitors nervous.

They'd barged upon the scene with a bodacious promise of bigger, better, fresher and priced right, and then delivered on it. *Burger Heaven* burgers, fries, chili and shakes really were great but it was the bold and innovative promotion during their launch that sealed the deal:

No Questions, No Fooling. 100% Money Back Guarantee if you don't love 'em!

Incredibly, reported the food industry and business press, almost no one took them up on it. Achieving unrivalled customer loyalty in record time, *Burger Heaven* now owned the market.

Prepping burgers in back, Sam Alman hated the place and

the moral decadence it stood for, but for a few more hours, until his mission was completed, it was his job. He detested Ray, the pimply-faced American boy, his *boss*. He missed his home and family in Tehran.

The fatty beef and French fries left him queasy and a little dizzy. Thundering Oldies music gave him an agonizing headache. The big busted American girls racing to customers on roller blades with exposed midriffs in too short, too tight short-shorts appalled him. And nothing could have prepared him for the vile customers. Infidels and heathen blasphemers so typical of this evil, godless country, they shamelessly assaulted everything sacred to him.

He hated them all and was honored by his privileged opportunity to strike at them.

"Sammy, how ya doin' with the *Big-Guy* patties, dude?" Ray called to him walking by.

"Just a little longer, Ray," Sam answered, hiding his contempt and resenting the inappropriate familiar tone. His ID said Sam Alman but his real name was Salim al Maanha.

"Cool, I'll be back for them in a few minutes. We're sellin' the fuck out of 'em today."

Sam winced at the profanity, silently asking Allah again for the strength to endure it.

At last it was time.

The other employees were out front taking and filling orders.

Sam worked alone preparing patties on massive trays of *Big Guy Burgers* in waiting. The opposite counter had pallets of buns and containers of lettuce, tomatoes, pickles and onions stacked high.

The Old Dog's New Trick

From his jacket pocket he withdrew a heavy zip-loc baggie containing a small white box with a 10 ml vial of a clear liquid. Sam had no idea what it was. They'd presented it as a scientifically engineered substance to trigger a virulent food poisoning – completely harmless to him, he was assured, as long as he didn't ingest it. Little chance of that, Sam thought grimly. He was the one *Burger Heaven* employee who had never and *would never* enjoy a *Big-Guy*.

What his handlers, the terrorist cell in Orange County that had recruited him, failed to ever mention were the liquid's deadly contagious properties. Or that any contact with his skin posed a problem he was better off not knowing about.

The instructions they'd given him were simple but quite specific.

"Replace the top with the rubber dropper and turn it over; it will deliver one drop at a time. Only one drop per patty is needed; after that move on to the buns and vegetables."

Sam worked quickly, recalling what came next. "Any remaining liquid should be used on the smaller hamburger patties for *Heavenly Kids Meals*." There was more than enough for the task. Finished, he returned the vial to the box and the box to the baggie. Sam's shift was almost over. *Insha'Allah*, he wouldn't return – ever.

Sam looked forward to his next assignment, certain of an even more worthy task. On his way home he'd dispose of the baggie as instructed.

They'd been quite specific about that, too.

*****

195

The old black dog lumbered slowly down the quiet residential street. At this early hour on Saturday morning there was no one about to engage him or shoo him away in the quiet old suburban neighborhood.

A people dog who had lost his people a few weeks ago, he was an English Labrador Retriever, not the taller and slender American Labs more common today. Where he came from, people routinely asked his owners what breed he was, unfamiliar with the fact that this was how the breed used to look. He possessed a huge blockhead, a thick barrel-chest and warm brown eyes still retaining a youthful zest that belied years not at all in doubt.

Scars on his legs and flanks hinted at surgeries, a distinguished silver muzzle and an explosion of gray now overrunning his belly and inner thighs at his age and, perhaps a scrap or two in his time. But he was a lover, not a fighter. The lab had a stunning medical file – the old guy had been loved by aging Baby Boomers who knew they would never be as medically fortunate when their own time came.

On a late spring camping vacation high in the Oregon Cascades, their burned bodies had been discovered in the Mount Hood National Forest east of Portland. A freak explosion of their camp stove ignited bone-dry timber needing little encouragement. It was lousy luck and a hideous death.

Driven off by the explosion the lab returned not long after, because wandering just wasn't his nature. The dog's life wasn't just *with them,* it *was them* – he was totally dedicated to his people. Confused and distraught, their devoted friend spent the rest of the day beside their bodies, never straying far, whimpering and keening.

The Old Dog's New Trick

Without understanding *why* he knew his life had changed forever.

A Park Ranger making the rounds of the campsite after the fire discovered the bodies and Sheriff's Deputies arrived early the next day. Spooked by all the sudden activity, the lab took to the hills and began his journey. Weeks later when he returned to civilization he was some twenty pounds lighter with muddy, crusted blood on his chest courtesy of a raccoon that, he'd learned the hard way, really didn't want to play after all.

He'd managed to find his way down out of the mountains to Portland, crossing the city and making his way to the West Hills where enclaves of forest and prestigious real estate separated city from suburbs. Now, having returned to civilization, he sought food, a place to sleep and human companionship.

He was lonely and missed people.

Garbage had been collected the previous day in this pleasant older part of the city so the pickings were slim. His world of new smells was limited to trees and shrubbery, the sidewalk and street. He sniffed it all in earnest, learning who'd been about and was marking territory when a big, middle-aged man in a hooded University of Oregon sweatshirt, running shoes and Blazers athletic shorts reaching nearly to his knees, rounded the corner at the end of the block.

For Ellroy "Cups" Drayton, an un-retired FBI agent, the early morning walk was the cardio component of a daily exercise regimen after a mild heart attack he'd suffered a little over a year before. His preference was pounding miles on a treadmill at 24 Hour Fitness but he spent weekends at Evie McClary's and on those days skipped the gym; opting instead for brisk walks through peaceful residential neighborhoods challenged by occasionally stout hills.

Cups grinned seeing the big black dog lifting his leg over Evie's prized flower beds, blissfully unaware he had company. Then, catching human scent and whirling around pressing low to the ground in prone position, the dog eyed him warily; he was on alert but also seemed ready to play.

"Are you lost, boy?" Cups asked.

Cups didn't recall ever seeing this dog before and thought he was really quite a handsome guy. A closer look as he approached revealed wherever he'd been, he'd really been through it. His ribs showed clearly. He desperately needed a bath and a good brushing. The dog remained still except for his impressive tail swishing hopefully in the grass.

"Got a tag, fella?" As Cups stepped towards him, the dog hopped back, eyes darting around in search of an escape route. Cups stopped and remained still, pausing briefly before speaking in a low, soft, unthreatening voice.

"No need to be afraid of me; it's okay. Come here – I'll scratch your belly."

The dog was torn. He wanted to come to Cups but couldn't; showing his dilemma by taking a tentative step or two before changing his mind and jumping back, whining, shaking his head and circling slowly at a safe distance. All the while his massive tail never stopped wagging and he never stopped smiling.

This dog had a great smile.

Cups decided to alter his tactics and try a different approach. "Think I'll sit and rest a bit. Maybe you'll change your mind. I can tell you're a good boy," he said, and sat down.

The Old Dog's New Trick

The dog cocked his head to one side as if he were listening. He decided to lie down, too. With his muzzle between his front paws, his tail was whipping so feverishly through the grass that Cups half expected him to lift off the ground. Appearing to further consider his options, the puzzled look on his face was soon replaced by one of single-minded interest. The dog rose and approached, closing half the distance between them before stopping.

"Good boy," Cups encouraged calmly, slowly extending the back of his hand towards him. No longer fearful, the dog launched himself at Cups, nearly knocking the big man over as he rushed to shower him with feverish doggie kisses while he wriggled as only a deliriously happy canine can. Cups scratched behind the dog's right ear. The lab groaned deeply, a hind leg scratching his side reflexively as he proceeded to lick Cups' face with purpose.

"Where've you been, boy? Looks to me like on the road quite a while. Bet you've got a story or two to tell, don't you?"

When the ear scratching stopped the dog rolled to his back and Cups moved to his belly. As Cups started to rise, slowly hauling his solid 6' 3" frame to his feet, the dog seemingly had a change of heart, panicked and bolted down the driveway. In a flash he had rounded the corner and was no longer in sight.

Nice old guy, Cups thought and sighed disappointedly. Sure hope he finds his way home.

Inside the house, breakfast was nearly ready. Evie loved cooking something special for him on weekend mornings. Today it was bacon, eggs and apple-cinnamon French toast. She bought the bread at Beaverton Bakery and sprinkled it with powdered sugar. With butter and maple syrup Cups swore it was the best he'd ever tasted. He no longer complained about the turkey bacon and Healthy Choice spread she substituted for butter, reluctantly accepting his new dietary fate that doctors had imposed and Evie diligently enforced.

"Do you want to eat or shower first?" She asked, wiping her brow and leaving a little powdered sugar low on her forehead.

Cups noticed her thick auburn curls had escaped the pony tail holder that only tenuously contained them. Her warm, green eyes had that vivid, electric sparkle that never failed to drive him wild.

"Let's eat, if you don't mind. I'll clean-up after breakfast," he answered pleasantly. "But first let me help you with something," and he brought her into his arms, kissing her eyebrows after wiping off the sugar.

Blushing, Evie smiled. "I'm incapable of spending time in the kitchen without getting whatever I'm making all over me! By the way, who were you talking to outside? I looked out but didn't see anyone."

Cups chuckled. "I interrupted a big old black lab watering your begonias. Nice old guy. Think he's lost, looked real road weary to me. Tried not to frighten him but he ran off."

Cups couldn't quite hide his disappointment. He loved dogs but Layla, Evie's aging tabby cat, was her baby so he never broached the subject; it just wasn't the time. Then their quiet morning was interrupted by a sudden thump against the kitchen door and the sound of Evie's watering can skittering across the redwood deck.

Evie looked out to see what had made the noise.

"Well, well, well," she said softly, an amused tone in her voice. "This could get interesting."

"What is it?" Cups asked.

"Your new friend is back," she smiled, "why don't you invite him in?"

I hope you enjoyed the Old Dog Preview.
To keep reading or learn more,
please visit my website:

www.PleaseReadMyBookBeforeIDie.com

19355200R10121

Made in the USA
San Bernardino, CA
22 February 2015